EDUCATION, RACISM AND REFORM

In this introductory text, Barry Troyna and Bruce Carrington look closely at widely-held assumptions about 'race' and schooling in Britain, and evaluate the role of the school in a multi-ethnic society. Focusing on contemporary issues and concerns, they consider such controversial questions as: Is the education system rigged against black pupils? Is 'tolerance' really a characteristic of the British? Is anti-racist education simply a 'loony tune' of the Left?

The authors provide a detailed analysis of the Education Reform Act (1988) and the debate surrounding the National Curriculum, and ask whether these new initiatives do truly open the doors of opportunity for all our children. In particular, they look critically at the Conservative government's claim that the National Curriculum will 'be helpful in holding together a multiracial and multicultural society'.

Lively and provocative, and covering the most recent developments in this area, *Education, Racism and Reform* will be of interest to students of education, teachers and to students on social science courses.

EDUCATION IN SOCIETY SERIES
Edited by Stephen J. Ball

Sex Roles and the School
2nd edition

Sara Delamont

EDUCATION, RACISM AND REFORM

Barry Troyna and
Bruce Carrington

London and New York

First published 1990
by Routledge
11 New Fetter Lane, London EC4P 4EE

Simultaneously published in the USA and Canada
by Routledge
a division of Routledge, Chapman and Hall, Inc.
29 West 35th Street, New York, NY 10001

©1990 B. Troyna and B. Carrington
Typeset by Witwell Ltd, Southport
Printed in Great Britain by
T.J. Press (Padstow) Ltd, Padstow, Cornwall.

British Library Cataloguing in Publication Data
Troyna, Barry
    Education, racism and reform. – (Education in society)
    1. Great Britain. Schools. Racism
    I. Title II. Carrington, Bruce III. Series
    370.19342

    ISBN 0-415-03825-1
        0-415-03826-X

Library of Congress Cataloging in Publication Data
Troyna, Barry.
        Education, racism and reform / Barry Troyna, Bruce Carrington.
        p.   cm. – (Education in society)
        Includes bibliographical references (p.   ).
        ISBN 0-415-03825-1. – ISBN 0-415-03826-X
        1. Education and state–Great Britain. 2. Minorities–Education–
Great Britain. 3. Racism–Great Britain. 4. Discrimination in
education–Great Britain. 5. Intercultural education–Great
Britain. I. Carrington, Bruce, 1948–   . II. Title. III. Series.
LC93.G7T65   1990
370′.941–dc20   89–49687
                                                              CIP

Contents

Series editor's preface

Of the wide range of issues confronting teachers at the present time, racism (in education and society) is probably the most controversial and divisive. It is also probably the most difficult, in the sense of knowing in realistic, practical terms what to do about it. But racism and racial inequality also confront us all with fundamental dilemmas of conscience: the personal and the political are tightly interrelated. If we do not stand out against racism wherever it occurs then are we not conniving with it?

The important thing is that the divisiveness, the dilemmas and the difficulty are not reasons for doing nothing. They make considered action all the more important. They indicate the need to be clear about what is happening, about the 'facts' of the matter, and the need for care in establishing a firm personal stance. For educators, clarity and sincerity are crucial.

This book, aimed at beginning teachers, attempts to clear the ground for considered action. Troyna and Carrington, both with long experience of working with schools that are engaged in anti-racist practice and with student teachers, present a committed and carefully argued case for anti-racist education. Their concerns and arguments are directly pertinent to both teachers in ethnically-mixed schools and those in the 'white highlands'. Their analysis and their questions demand to be taken seriously.

Stephen J. Ball

Acknowledgements

We would like to thank Stephen Ball for asking (or was it telling?) us to write this book for his series. Arman Alan Ali, Director of Greater London Action for Race Equality, Andrew Dorn, of the Commission for Racial Equality, and Heather Lynn, Librarian at the Centre for Research in Ethnic Relations at the University of Warwick, provided us with a range of important documentation. Liz Carrington and Sue Tall did a splendid job of word-processing the manuscript and compensating for our Luddite inclinations. Thanks also to Jayne Mills and Sharon Gewitz for their help in the preparation of the book.

I am grateful to Wendy Ball, Richard Hatcher and Pat Sikes, colleagues at the University of Warwick, for their constructive comments about some of the arguments that are raised in the book, and to my fellow governors and the staff at Edgewick community primary school in Coventry for helping me to understand the realities of the ERA at the chalk face. Above all, thanks to dad: a real *mensch*; and to mum: my memories of you continue to inspire. (BT)

Thanks to Tony Edwards, Anna Duffy, Carol Fitz-Gibbon and Christine Skelton for making my sabbatical feasible; to Geoffrey Short for his many helpful suggestions; and to Liz, Alex and Rebecca for their continuing support. (BC)

Barry Troyna
Bruce Carrington

Introduction

In this book, we provide a critical perspective on the literature and debates about racial inequality and education. Focusing on contemporary issues and concerns in the UK, we explore various assumptions about the role of the school in a multi-cultural society and highlight some of the shortcomings of policy and research on this topic. We consider also the case for anti-racist education and examine its prospects in the light of the Education Reform Act (1988) and the emerging National Curriculum. Central to our analysis is the conviction that anti-racist education, contrary to the claims of its detractors, is fully compatible with what many would regard as a 'good' education.

What is anti-racist education? What are its central concepts and concerns and how do these differ from those of multi-cultural education? We have argued elsewhere (e.g. Carrington and Troyna 1988) that anti-racist education refers to a wide range of organizational, curricular and pedagogical strategies which aim to promote racial equality and to eliminate attendant forms of discrimination and oppression, both individual and institutional. Such reforms involve a reappraisal of both the hidden and the formal curriculum. In the case of the hidden curriculum, anti-racists have called for: the recruitment of more black teachers (especially to promoted positions); more effective measures to counter cultural bias in assessment and selection procedures; initiatives to extend parental and pupil involvement in decisions about the organization and priorities of schooling; and the development of strategies and policies to deal with racist harassment. Anti-racists have also stressed the need for the democratization of schooling and for changes in the formal curriculum to include explicit teaching against racism and other forms of injustice. In Chapters 1 and 3, we shall provide a detailed analysis of the concept of racism and will explore the research on the racial attitudes and behaviour of children and young people. We shall also outline some of the principles which might underpin curricular initiatives to combat racism and will show how these have been put into operation in a range of educational settings.

This conception of education in a multicultural society is light years away from the 'monocultural' or 'immigrant' educational ideologies which prevailed in the 1960s and 1970s and which continue to feature on the educational landscape. The message which these convey to ethnic minority pupils is loud and clear: forget the culture of your parents, discard any affiliation to your ethnic background and blend in. 'Being British in this version', argue Cashmore and Troyna (1990:8), 'is instead of, not as well as, being an ethnic group member. It's one-way: acquisition involves loss.' However, while there is a clear distinction between these ideologies and anti-racism, there are some who view anti-racist versions of educational reform as different only in tenor from multicultural education. Consider, for instance, Bhikhu Parekh's claim that anti-racist education is 'in substance little different from multicultural education' (Parekh 1986:30). Can this assertion be sustained?

Along with Richard Hatcher (1987), we insist that there are fundamental theoretical differences between anti-racists and multiculturalists. These are particularly evident in their respective conceptualizations of culture and racism. Although both anti-racists and multiculturalists recognize the need for schools to celebrate cultural diversity in the curriculum, the concept of culture in the discourse of multiculturalism, as Hatcher has pointed out, is 'given only a taken-for-granted commonsense meaning, impoverished both theoretically and in terms of concrete lived experience' (Hatcher 1987:188). For instance, multiculturalists largely ignore the influence of social class on attitudes, beliefs and behaviour. Criticisms can also be levelled against multiculturalists' approaches to racism, which tend to conflate racism with prejudice. They portray racism as little more than a form of intolerance which stems from an individual's irrationality and ignorance. Seen through the lens of anti-racist education, this is a distorted and simplistic understanding of racism. 'Racism is not an individual problem,' writes Barb Thomas, 'it is lodged squarely in the policies, structures, practices and beliefs of everyday life' (Thomas 1984:24). Despite what Parekh and others might say, there continues to be important differences between multiculturalists and anti-racists. When the former deal with culture and racism, the emphasis is squarely on 'them'. The priority is to provide information which is expected to dislodge white children's negative and stereotypical views of ethnic minority cultures. For anti-racists, the attention is focused on 'us'. Here, emphasis is placed on the development of strategies which help children to probe 'the manner in which racism rationalises and helps maintain injustice and the differential power accorded groups in society' (Troyna 1989:182).

Deconstructing the obvious

In April 1980, Professor Stuart Hall, now of the Open University, gave an informal talk to the London branch of the Association of Teachers of Social Science (ATSS). The talk was entitled 'Teaching Race' and an edited transcript was published subsequently in the now defunct journal, *Multiracial Education* (Hall 1980). Hall's talk was a *tour de force*, a seminal contribution to debates about how anti-racist education might best be conceived and implemented. Although Hall dealt only fleetingly with what the substantive content of the intervention might look like, his analysis of how teachers might tackle racism in schools and classrooms remains unassailable in our view, as our published work in this area testifies (e.g. Carrington and Troyna 1988). Nor would we wish to underestimate the influence of Hall's analysis on our roles as anti-racist teachers, researchers and school governors.

In the course of his talk, Hall alluded to the part that social science might play in helping people to interpret and make sense of the world. He put it like this: 'Social science is about deconstructing the obvious, it is about showing people that the things they immediately feel to be "just like that" aren't quite "just like that" ' (Hall 1980:6). In this short, pithy sentence,

Hall captures what we see as the aims of this book: to undermine the obvious and to encourage critical scrutiny of some of the main, taken-for-granted assumptions about 'race' and schooling. What are these assumptions, these articles of faith, which have naturalized themselves and become almost impervious to change? We have identified three.

First, there is the pervasive and enduring belief that black pupils, especially those of Afro-Caribbean origin, consistently perform less well than white indigenous pupils in examinations. Linked to this is the more insidious proposition that this differential in examination performance derives less from inequity in school (expressed in a range of manifest forms) than from the deficiencies of Afro-Caribbean cultural and family norms and values. In Chapter 2 we shall look closely at this debate and show that the Swann committee, which in 1985 reported the findings of its inquiry into the education of children from ethnic minority groups, gave its blessing to this racist interpretation of 'black underachievement'.

The second article of faith relates to the nature and extent of racism in the UK. In the words of Douglas Hurd, the then Home Secretary, 'freedom of speech and expression and the toleration of different opinions are ideals to which the British people are firmly committed' (Hurd 1989). Those who dissent from such principles, according to this argument, are in the minority and have stepped beyond the normal conventions which govern life in the UK. This 'rotten apple theory of racism', as Julian Henriques (1984) calls it, figures prominently in objections to the development of anti-racist education. However, as we shall demonstrate in Chapter 1 and more extensively in Chapter 3, this liberal understanding of racism bears little resemblance to reality.

Finally, we shall centre attention on the third article of faith: the 1988 Education Reform Act (ERA) and the administrative, systemic, financial and curricular changes that it prescribes. In the words of its main architect, Kenneth Baker, the ERA will 'open the doors of opportunity [not] slam them in front of our children' (Baker 1987:8). By centralizing terms such as 'choice, freedom, standards and quality control', in his public present-ation of the provisions of the ERA, and by characterizing the

National Curriculum as an 'entitlement curriculum', Baker's assurances would seem to have a genuine ring about them. We have our doubts, however. In Chapters 4, 5 and 6 we shall engage critically with this interpretation of the ERA, outline what we see as its confining effects on racial equality in education, and suggest some counter-strategies. Let us begin, however, by considering responses to anti-racist initiatives in education.

1   Anti-racist education:
a loony tune?

As we enter the 1990s it is becoming increasingly 'obvious' to a growing number of people that anti-racist education (ARE) is a 'loony tune' of the radical left; another antic of 'the race lobby' which, as the *Daily Mail* insists, flies in the face of 'common sense' ('More anti-racist nonsense', *Daily Mail*, 17 May 1989). Burnage High School in Manchester, Highbury Quadrant primary school in London, Brent, Dewsbury and the Inner London education authorities have assumed demonic status in the eyes of the anti-anti-racists. This group of critics is not confined to right-wing theorists and activists. On the contrary, its membership is expanding at an inexorable rate and largely transcends conventional left/right, professional/non-professional divisions in the educational community. Therefore, let us examine the objections to ARE. At the risk of over-simplification, they seem to crystallize around three discernible, if not entirely independent nor discrete, issues: its mismanagement and application; its principles; and its irrelevance.

The first objection figures prominently in the critiques of (some) radical and liberal commentators on ARE. For instance, James Lynch, a leading exponent of cultural pluralist ideas, castigates ARE for being 'too political, confrontational, accusatory and guilt-inducing' (Lynch 1987:x). The National Union of Teachers tends to agree. In its guidelines on anti-racism in education, it concedes that there have been 'insensitive applications of anti-racist policies in some areas' (NUT 1989:1). Indeed, this constituted the main criticism in the report of the MacDonald inquiry into the murder of Ahmed Iqbal Ullah by a white pupil, Darren Coulbourn, in the playground of Burnage High School in 1986. Whilst the committee of inquiry voiced its

LIFE CAN BE SO NICE

support for policies to tackle racism in education, it criticized the senior management of Burnage for applying a simplistic model of anti-racism to the school in their forlorn attempt to manage the tensions that were generated by the murder. As the committee observed, 'the application of a moral antiracism' which assumes that all whites are racist was 'an unmitigated disaster' which exacerbated rather than defused tensions in the school (MacDonald *et al.* 1989). Along the same lines has been the assessment of how Brent LEA in London has proceeded to tackle racism in its local schools. The HMI reports into educational provision in Brent (HMI 1987) and, in the following year, the authority's Development Programme for Race Equality (DPRE) (HMI 1988), alongside Sir David Lane's report on the DPRE for the Home Office (Lane 1988), coalesce around criticisms of the vigorous, some might say philistine, way in which the LEA has attempted to put flesh on the bones of its anti-racist education policy. The dispute that centred on the alleged racist remarks made by a local primary headteacher, Maureen McGoldrick, in 1986, the setting up in the same year of the DPRE – a group of advisers who were typified in the media as 'race spies' – and the comings and goings of Directors of Education generated considerable and prolonged media attention and criticism. Reactions to the events at Highbury Quadrant school in Islington also fit into this category. The decision to hold an assembly there in July 1988 to celebrate Nelson Mandela's 70th birthday sparked off a chain of events which culminated in the ILEA deciding to remove experienced teachers from the school. Once again, this stemmed from a perception of overzealous involvement of the school's senior management in implementing anti-racist policies. 'The Highbury Quadrant teachers regarded antiracism as something they could teach through their militancy,' insisted the Labour leader of the ILEA, Neil Fletcher. 'As an authority we would reject that' (*Guardian*, 13 December 1988).

Whilst these criticisms do not attack the legitimacy of ARE *per se*, there are those who have raised doubts about the efficacy of its principles and have questioned their relevance to the educational experiences of black (and white) pupils. This was expressed most vividly at the Conservative party's annual conference in 1987. There Mrs Thatcher juxtaposed ARE with 'good' education in her gratuitous claim that 'Children who need to be able to count and multiply are learning anti-racist mathematics – whatever that may be' (Thatcher 1987). Others have indicated, in less hysterical terms, that a concern with ARE might be diversionary, inhibiting rather than enhancing the academic progress of black pupils. For this reason, Malcolm Cross (1989) is critical of anti-racists who have mounted 'thoughtless attacks' on the National Curriculum. In his view, the revival of 'core' subjects in the new legislation could provide a 'window of opportunity' for black pupils who, for one reason or another, have been deprived of the educational experiences that are enjoyed by their white, middle-class counterparts. Circumstantial support for Cross comes from an inquiry into the London borough of Newham, where examination results are notoriously low and where ARE features prominently on the educational landscape. According to the chair of the inquiry team, Seamus Hegarty, the LEA has given more attention to raising teachers' awareness of racism than to meeting the needs of black pupils. Put another way, ARE has benefited white teachers more than black pupils, enhancing the career opportunities of the former whilst depressing those of the latter (*Independent*, 7 April 1989).

Criticism of the management, relevance and efficacy of ARE has thus loomed large in the campaign of vilification. None the less, the most trenchant objections to ARE have been voiced by those polemicists and theorists who are associated with the New Right. Since the mid-1980s, ARE has been subjected to unrelenting attacks by Anthony Flew, Ray Honeyford, the Hillgate Group, Frank Palmer, Roger Scruton, John Marks and other doyens of the New Right. They challenge the very *raison d'être* of ARE (see Oldman 1987). Their interventions have rested on two main predicates. First, in contradistinction to compaigners for ARE, they insist that racism is neither institutionalized nor normative in British society (e.g. Honeyford 1988). In other words, they subscribe to what we saw referred to earlier as the 'rotten apple theory of racism'. Second, they perceive the function of schooling largely in instrumental terms. In this view, 'the deterioration in British education has arisen partly because schools have been treated as instruments for equalizing, rather than instructing, children' (Hillgate Group 1987:2). The educational (and social) policy that stems logically from a synthesis of these positions corresponds with interpretations of the liberal democratic tradition. The state should offer protection to individual liberties and therefore must try to ensure that black pupils are not subjected to explicit forms of racial discrimination and violence. In addition, the state, where necessary, should provide black pupils with the opportunity to become functionally competent in English. However, no other concessions are necessary and should not be offered. In short, black pupils should be treated as 'trainee whites'. The assimilationist approach that this commends has characterized some of the responses to Muslim objections to Salman Rushdie's *The Satanic Verses*. It will be recalled that, closely associated with fundamentalist demands for the banning of this book, there was a more forceful insistence, on the part of some Muslim community spokespersons, for separate schools. The media and public response demonstrated unequivocally that assimilationism, and the conditional citizenship for blacks which it implies, was once again in the ascendancy. As Woodrow Wyatt, 'the voice of reason' in the *News of the World*, put it to his readers:

> newcomers here are welcome. But only if they become genuine Britishers and don't stuff their alien cultures down our throats.
>
> (5 March 1989)

Or as George Gale, 'cutting through the nonsense' and presenting 'the voice of common sense', informed his *Daily Mail* readership under the headline, 'No room for aliens':

> we must do nothing through legislation or the use of public money to preserve alien cultures and religions. Likewise, they must seek to be assimilated. . . . They have chosen to dwell amongst us. In Rome, do as the Romans do.
>
> (3 March 1989)

For those who have first-hand experience of the changing political climate in the 'race' and schooling debate, from the time when black pupils first began to make their presence felt in the UK's schools in the early 1960s, the influence of the New Right's conception of 'the multicultural society' on national and local policy in the late 1980s provides a sense of *déjà vu*: a flashback to the days, nearly thirty years ago, when 'only if' definitions of citizenship for black immigrants and their children prevailed. Consider, for example, the close resemblance between the views of Wyatt and Gale and those of George Partiger (former MP for Southall) who had this to say in 1964:

> I feel that Sikh parents should encourage their children to give up their turbans, their religion and their dietary laws. If they refuse to integrate then we must be tough. They must be told that they would be the first to go if there was unemployment and it should be a condition of being given National Assistance that the immigrants go to English classes.

(cited in Troyna 1982:129)

Nor are the similarities confined to media discourse or political rhetoric. The re-emergence of assimilation as a credible and legitimate ideological base for the debate about 'race' and schooling can also be inferred from the framing of recent policy documents. Of these, the education development plan that was issued by the Royal Borough of Kensington and Chelsea springs to mind. In 1988 the borough declared its intention to abandon ARE principles and practices when it assumes responsibility for local services from the ILEA in April 1990. Its education plan, issued in early 1989, actualized this commitment. Thus, after a perfunctory acknowledgement of the borough's duties under Section 71 of the 1976 Race Relations Act, which the borough conceives in the narrow sense of promoting 'equality of opportunity' rather than the broader commitment to 'eliminate unlawful racial discrimination', the plan proceeds to identify the 'specific educational needs' of ethnic minority pupils (Royal Borough 1989:49). However, these are defined in terms of, and confined to, language, with an assurance that the borough will help pupils whose mother tongue is not English to develop competence in this language. The value of mother-tongue teaching is also interpreted in these terms; namely, as a means to an end – the acquisition of English. The limited conception of ethnic minority 'needs' in the borough can also be inferred from the decision to locate responsibility for 'multi-ethnic needs', at inspectorate level, with the Inspector for Communication and to diffuse the concern for promoting equality of opportunity throughout the inspectorate without any indication of how this might be monitored (Royal Borough 1989:49).

The policy proposals of the Royal Borough of Kensington and Chelsea constitute a most spectacular retreat from ARE principles and interpretations. However, the borough is not alone. Other LEAs, such as Berkshire, Bradford, Inner London and Manchester, have demonstrated, in recent years and in different ways, a more hesitant and ambivalent commitment to ARE in particular and to egalitarian initiatives in general. Whilst 'colour-blindness' has not been reinstated as a policy imperative in these LEAs, the radical approach to the formulation, implementation and appraisal of ARE, which characterized their procedures in the mid-1980s, is now a thing of the past (Troyna and Williams 1986).

The liberal moment thus seems to have gone. That moment started with the publication of the 1977 Green Paper, *Education in Schools: A Consultative Document*, where for the first time the DES acknowledged, albeit in the most tentative manner, the legitimacy of cultural pluralist conceptions of educational reform:

> Our society is a multicultural, multiracial one and the curriculum should reflect a sympathetic understanding of the different cultures and races [*sic*] that now make up our society.
>
> (DES 1977:41)

The pursuit of egalitarian reforms, especially from anti-racist perspectives, gained momentum with the outbreak of urban disorders in 1980, 1981 and 1985 (see Chapter 2) and ended, in our view, with the introduction of the Great Education Reform Bill (GERBIL) into the House of Commons in November 1987. We can now look back with some nostalgia on that period, which saw an increasing awareness of how racial and gender inequalities disfigure the educational life-chances of pupils and which encouraged a number of LEAs and their schools to promote ARE (and other egalitarian initiatives) as an integral and informing aspect of their policy and practice. Of course, we should not romanticize this trend; after all, there were some LEAs and institutions where ARE constituted little more than impression-management and the great divide between rhetoric and practice was never seriously broached, never mind breached (Troyna and Ball 1985). At the same time, it would be disingenuous not to acknowledge some of the important steps that were taken at local government level and in some schools and colleges towards expediting provision and resources for the development of strategic policies to combat racism (alongside other structural inequalities) and the practices to which they give rise.

The shifting sands of ideology and policy

How do we make sense of the changing ideological and policy idioms in the 'race' and schooling debate? As Table 1.1 indicates, there has been a range of initiatives in this sphere of educational and social policy since the early 1960s and we have given some flavour of the rapidly changing ways in which the issues have been defined and, in some cases, confined. These 'racial forms of education', according to Chris Mullard, have assumed various guises: 'immigrant', 'multiracial', 'multicultural' and most recently, of course, anti-racist education (Mullard 1984:14). However, these labels tell us little about the political or educational principles which underpinned the policy and pedagogical approaches. It is important, therefore, to go beyond the historical narrative that is provided by Sally Tomlinson (1983) and the Swann committee (DES 1985a) and to consider the conceptual frameworks which social scientists have generated not simply to trace, but also to understand, the evolution of policy and practice on 'race' and education over the last twenty-five years.

For many writers in the field, the most compelling and plausible interpretations of these changes appear in the work of Street-Porter (1978), Mullard (1982) and Troyna (1982), who draw on analytical tools which are provided by the sociology of

Table 1.1 The educational response to black pupils in British schools and related policy initiatives on 'race', 1962–89

	Legislation	Education policy and government publications	Action and events
1962	Commonwealth Immigrants Act		Commonwealth Immigrants Advisory Council set up
1963		Ministry of Education agrees to the 'dispersal' of 'immigrant' children; publishes *English for Immigrants*	
1964			Bipartism policy on 'race' and immigration begins
1965	Race Relations Act	DES Circular 7/65 sanctions 'dispersal'; White Paper on immigration published	Race Relations Board set up
1966	Section 11 of the Local Government Act	DES starts to collect statistics on 'immigrant children'	Local authorities with substantial numbers of 'immigrants' become eligible to apply for Section 11 funds; School Council project, *English for Immigrant Children*, begins (finishes 1973)

Table 1.1 continued

	Legislation	Education policy and government publications	Action and events
1967		Plowden Report sets up EPAs: the presence of immigrants in need of ESL is regarded as a criterion for defining an EPA	Political and Economic Planning report on racial discrimination published; Schools Council project, *Teaching English to West Indian Children*, begins (finishes 1973)
1968	Commonwealth Immigrants Act; Race Relations Act	Urban Aid Programme announced; funds to be made available to 'urban areas of general needs'	Community Relations Commission set up; Enoch Powell makes his 'rivers of blood' speech
1969	Local Government Grants (Social Need) Act marks the start of the Urban Aid Programme		Section 11 grants increased; Townsend and Brittan begin DES-funded research at the NFER (completed 1972)
1971	Immigration Act	DES Surveys 10, *Potential and Progress in a Second Culture*, and 13, *The Education of Immigrants*, published	Bernard Coard's *How the West Indian Child is Made ESN in the British School System* published
1972		DES Survey 14, *The Continuing Needs of Immigrants*, published	

1973	DES stops collecting 'immigrant' statistics; Report of the Select Committee on Race Relations and Immigration published, containing 24 recommendations for education	Schools Council project, *Education for a Multiracial Society*, begins (finishes 1976)
1974	DES *Educational Disadvantage and the Educational Needs of Immigrants* published in response to Select Committee report of 1973	Education Disadvantage Unit, Centre for Education Disadvantage, and Assessment of Performance Unit set up
1975	Bullock Committee of Inquiry's *Language of Life* published (ch. 20 dealing with children from families of overseas origin); White Paper, *Racial Discrimination*, published	

Table 1.1 continued

	Legislation	Education policy and government publications	Action and events
1976	Race Relations Act		Community Relations Commission and Race Relations Board replaced by Commission for Racial Equality; Murder of Gurdip Singh Chaddar
1977		Publication of: Report of Select Committee on Race Relations and Immigration, *The West Indian Community*; ILEA policy document, *Multiethnic Education*; DES Green Paper, *Education in Schools*	EEC issues a directive on the education of migrant workers' children, to come into force in 1981; Urban aid replaced by policy for inner-city areas inner-city areas
1978		Home Office puts out a White Paper, *The West Indian Community*, in response to Select Committee of 1977; DES circulates *Education in Schools: a Consultative Document*	Schools Council decides not to accept the report, *Education for a Multiracial Society*; Murder of Altab Ali; ALTARF formed

1979		Rampton committee starts to receive evidence; Little and Willey begin research at the Schools Council (published 1981)
1980	White Paper on nationality published	Centre for Educational Disadvantage closes in Manchester; 'Riots' in St Paul's, Bristol
1981	Publication of: House of Commons Home Affairs Committee's *Racial Disadvantage*; *Racial Attacks*, report of a Home Office study; Interim report of the Rampton committee, *West Indian Children in our Schools*	'Riots' at Brixton and Toxteth; Lord Swann replaces Anthony Rampton as chair of the Committee of Inquiry into the Education of Children from Ethnic Minority Groups; New version of Schools Council project report published
1982	Home Office Circular 97/82 revises the guidelines for Section 11 funds	

Table 1.1 continued

	Legislation	Education policy and government publications	Action and events
1983	House of Lords ruling on the definition of 'racial group', in Mandlas v. Dowell-Lee		CRE publishes *Secondary School Allocation in Reading*; ILEA publishes its six policy documents, *Race, Sex and Class*
1985		Swann report, *Education for All*, published	CRE publishes *Immigration Control Procedures* and *Birmingham LEA and Schools: Referral and Suspension of Pupils*; 'Riots' in Handsworth and Tottenham
1986	Education Act		Maureen McGoldrick affair in Brent; Bradford headteacher, Ray Honeyford, leaves with £160,000 golden handshake
1987		Education reform bill introduced in House of Commons (November); HMI report that Brent's anti-racist policy has 'a helpful effect on work in classrooms'	White parents in Dewsbury withdraw their children from multi-racial school; CRE report shows that Calderdale LEA has been discriminating against 'Asian' pupils

1988	Education Reform Act	HMI and Home Office publish reports on Brent	CRE publishes *Learning in Terror* and *Medical School Admissions*; Manchester City Council decides not to publish full report of the inquiry into Burnage School; Highbury Quadrant School, Islington criticized for holding an assembly celebrating Mandela's 70th birthday
1989		Home Office publishes the report of the Inter-Departmental Racial Attacks Group	NUT publishes *Anti-Racism in Education Guidelines*; Campaign for Anti-Racist Education (CARE) formed

race relations. They specify ideological and policy approaches in terms of assimilation, integration and cultural pluralism. These phases are periodized from the early 1960s through to the mid-1980s, although they are intended neither to imply a neat and regular progression nor to denote practices at the 'chalk face'. Their intention is to characterize prevailing ideologies as they are reflected in the rhetoric and policy prescriptions at national and local government level. Each ideological concept embodies a specific 'racial form of education' and, according to some writers (e.g. Jeffcoate 1984), denotes particular perceptions and conceptions of the relationship between black pupils and the state. This was not the view of Mullard or Troyna, however. They argued that the move towards cultural pluralist models of education did not constitute a significant departure from the assumptions and principles which underpinned assimilationist conceptions. That is to say, multicultural education, although representing a more liberal variant of the assimilationist model, continued to draw its inspiration and rationale from white, middle-class, professional understandings of how the educational system might best respond to the perceived 'needs' and 'interests' of black students and their parents. Thus, whichever of these paradigms was in the ascendancy, the power relationship between black and white citizens remained unchallenged. The focus of concern was cultural differences and the extent to which these were regarded as inhibiting the educational careers and experiences of black students. When this concern was translated into policy and curriculum imperatives, it assumed the form of what Troyna called the Three S's approach: Saris, Samosas and Steel bands (Troyna and Williams 1986:24). In other words, there was a determination to ensure that the lifestyles of black pupils were reflected (and respected) in curriculum models and teaching materials. This belief in the causal relationship between the promotion of lifestyles and the enhancement of life-chances for black pupils was seductive, enduring and non-threatening. Indeed the definitive link in the policy approaches to which these paradigms gave rise, was the absence of any sustained consideration of the impact of racism on black students' differential access to, experiences in, and outcomes from, the educational system.

A second analytical approach was developed by the American sociologist, David Kirp, in his controversial book *Doing Good by Doing Little* (1979). Kirp dichotomized ideological and policy responses into 'racially inexplicit' and 'racially explicit' formulations. These terms comprised both descriptive and evaluative elements. At the time of writing he viewed the policy approach in the UK, definitively, as 'racially inexplicit'. This was in sharp contrast to policy formulations in the USA where, since 1954 (when the Supreme Court had ruled that segregated education was unconstitutional), 'race' had been a salient item on the educational policy agenda. Kirp argued that, since the Supreme Court's ruling, racial inequality had constituted a fulcrum around which policy interventions in the USA had been framed. In the UK, on the other hand, and with the conspicuous exception of the policies relating to the dispersal (or 'bussing') of black students in some LEAs (see Killian 1979), race-related matters had not figured explicitly as policy concerns. Instead, their significance had been embedded in a range of 'racially inexplicit' categories such as language provision, educational disadvantage, cultural deprivation and cultural adjustment. It was within these broadly conceived categories that policy-makers had decided to tackle the problems associated with black students. At a descriptive level, Kirp's account could not be faulted. Where we take issue is with his *evaluation* of the approach that was adopted by UK policy-makers. For him, this deliberately inadvertent strategy could be regarded as 'doing good by stealth'. He insisted that such an approach had much to commend it because it did not contravene the principles of universalism and individualism which underpin educational policy in the UK; namely, 'we treat all children the same' whilst 'recognising (and responding to) the particular needs of individual pupils'. What is more, Kirp argued, by diffusing race-related initiatives through this more broadly conceived approach, policy-makers forestalled the likelihood of a 'white backlash'. As Kirp maintained: 'one helps non-whites by *not* favouring them explicitly. The benefits to minorities from such an approach are thought to be real if invisible – or better, real because invisible' (Kirp 1979:51; original emphasis).

Kirp's commitment to the ideology of doing good by doing

little has been criticized for its failure to recognize how 'inexplicitness', by its very nature, precludes any engagement with the impact of racism on black students' experiences. After all, it presumes that existing categories which define modes of policy intervention are capable of capturing and dealing with the full range of disadvantages experienced by young blacks. This is a spurious and sanguine argument. It denies the significance of racism on the lives and opportunities of these youngsters. The fundamental weakness of Kirp's appraisal is that it fails to conceive the education system as a site in which the reproduction of racism is achieved and confirmed. As such it does not engage with the most obvious of the demands that are expressed by black groups in the UK; that policy-makers develop approaches and forms of provision which acknowledge and tackle racism and the practices which stem from it. For Kirp to characterize this 'inexplicit' approach as 'good' is to disregard the voice of the black communities and to help to legitimate an educational system which contributes to their continued oppression and enforced inequality.

The third conception of how policy has evolved in the UK was developed by Troyna and Williams in *Racism, Education and the State* (1986). Building on the assimilation, integration, cultural pluralism typology, they suggested that the deracialization/racialization process which was defined and developed by Frank Reeves in 1983 might provide greater clarity and insight than the existing explanatory models. They argued that policies which were informed by assimilation, integration or cultural pluralism were classic examples of deracialized discourse. That is to say, policy-makers who had framed their policies along these lines had deliberately eschewed overt reference to racial descriptions, evaluations and prescriptions in preference to apparently more legitimate educational imperatives. Thus, from this perspective,

> the process of resocialisation, language tuition and correction and dispersal could be argued for on the seemingly 'good' educational grounds that the culture, language and spatial concentration of black students not only impeded their educational advancement but also had the potential to affect

negatively the educational progress of their white classmates.
(Troyna and Williams 1986:13)

Following on from this, Troyna and Williams suggested that
policy formulations – whether embedded in the ideological
framework of assimilation, integration or cultural pluralism –
were premised on the assumption that the priority was the
management of problems which were thrown up by the presence
of black students rather than the mitigation of problems which
black students encountered precisely because they were black
citizens living in a racist society. Thus, the package of reforms
that was introduced in the 1970s, which has come to be known as
multicultural education, concentrated on trying to ensure that the
schooling experiences of black students were made more pala-
table. The reforms were geared towards a representation of black
students' (presumed) lifestyles in curriculum design and teaching
aids. However, they ignored the formal and informal racist
processes which constrained the educational opportunities that
were available to these students. This, Troyna and Williams
concluded, was discrimination by proxy.

In contrast to these deracialized forms of discourse and
intervention was the (benign) racialization of educational policy
and debate. Following Reeves, Troyna and Williams suggested
that there were certain contexts where explicit use was made of
racial evaluations and categorizations and that these contexts
might be benign or malevolent. For example, ethnic record-
keeping in education would be designated as 'malevolent' if used
by the National Front for avowedly racist aims, or 'benign' if
used, say, by the Commission for Racial Equality for explicitly
anti-racist intentions.

Troyna and Williams contended that the trend towards the
publication of anti-racist education policies in the early-mid-
1980s, at local education authority level, represented a *benign*
form of racialization in that the policies reflected a growing
awareness of and indignation at racial injustice. In consequence,
'Racial evaluation and prescription is directed at refuting racism
and eliminating racialist practices' (Reeves 1983:175). For
Troyna and Williams, the deracialization/racialization framework provided the most perceptive and sensitive analytical

lens through which to observe and interpret the shifting sands of ideological and policy stances on race-related matters in education.

Deracialization and the New Right

As we have seen, educational policies to promote racial equality and justice have not only been vilified by the media, but also been disparaged elsewhere as subversive, irrelevant and inimical to 'good' educational practice. Increasingly, there have been calls for a return to the politics of assimilation. In all, this suggests that we are entering a new era of deracialization. How is this apparent policy shift to be interpreted?

As our analysis of recent events in Brent, at Highbury Quadrant School and at Burnage High School has shown, the media (especially the tabloid press) have played a crucial role in fostering public antipathy towards anti-racism and other egalitarian policies. Sensational and often grossly inaccurate reporting about such policies has helped to trigger a 'moral panic' (i.e. widespread feeling of unease, suspicion and consternation) about their implementation (Gordon and Rosenberg 1989). As a result of this 'moral panic', LEAs have been placed under considerable pressure either to abandon or to modify drastically their commitment to anti-racist principles and practices. Andrew Pollard has described this course of events as follows:

> the work or activity of a particular group – e.g. of antiracist teachers or of proponents of peace studies – comes to the attention of some people who are 'shocked' at what they see as a move outside normal boundaries of the curriculum or of practice. This is followed by public expressions of disquiet and gradually, often with amplification from the media, a sense of 'moral outrage' is generated whilst, at the same time, particular 'true values and traditions' are asserted by concerned interest groups. This puts the 'deviants' under considerable pressure and they are either isolated, marginalised or forced into conformity.

(Pollard 1988:57)

Right-wing thinking about 'race' relations has undergone several perceptible changes in recent years, especially in the wake of the urban disorders of 1980, 1981 and 1985. These changes have arisen as a result of a concerted effort by the New Right to create a popular alternative to the cultural pluralist and anti-racist perspectives of the Centre and Left. The plans of the Royal Borough of Kensington and Chelsea to pursue an educational policy which rests upon assimilationist principles must be seen in the light of such changes. As John Solomos has argued, there are a number of elements in New Right ideology on 'race' and 'nation' which 'can be said to signal new developments in the politics of racism as it has been constituted and reformed since the 1960s' (Solomos 1988:227). These elements are:

(a) the location of 'race' and 'nation' as historical invariables;
(b) a definition of national identity around powerful images of culture, way of life and the family; (c) the perception of blacks as an 'alien wedge'; and (d) the perception of 'race' as a major factor in explaining the growth of violence in British Society.

(Solomos 1988:227-8)

Solomos shows how, in the aftermath of urban unrest and disorder, New Right commentators have not only characterized black youth as 'violent hooligans', who are posing a threat to law and order, but also depicted black people as 'aliens' (with different values and traditions), who are posing a threat to the 'British way of life'. This virulent brand of assimilationism, as suggested by our discussion of the media and public response to Muslim objections to *The Satanic Verses*, may be commonplace in popular culture. In Solomos's view, the ideological construction of Afro-Caribbeans and South Asians as 'an alien wedge' in society has helped to legitimate the New Right's stereotypical perception of 'British culture' as monolithic and ethnically undifferentiated. He also points out that, by 'denying the possibility that black people can share the native population's attachment to the national culture', this specious conception of British culture effectively 'rationalises the exclusion of black people from equal participation in social institutions' (Solomos 1988:230). In other words, it renders anti-racist policies irrelevant.

Similar concerns have been voiced by Steve Randall (1988). To highlight the simplistic nature of the concept of 'British culture' in the discourse of the New Right, he draws attention to the 'working definition' that was provided by John Casey (1982), in the first edition of *The Salisbury Review*, the journal of 'conservative thought'. Echoing T. S. Eliot, Casey suggested that 'British culture'

> includes all the characteristic activities and interests of a people: Derby Day, Henley Regatta, Cowes, the twelfth of August, a cup-final, the dog races, the pin table, the dart board, Wensleydale cheese, boiled cabbage cut into sections, beetroot in vinegar, nineteenth century gothic churches and the music of Elgar.
>
> (see Randall 1988:8)

By focusing on these arbitary and more obvious facets of lived experience, Casey is able both to trivialize the effects of social class differences on lifestyles, and to ignore the influence of other salient divisions: that is, those based on ethnic, gender, regional and national differences. His conception of 'British culture' is nothing more than a glib and sentimental celebration of what might possibly be regarded as quintessentially English.

An impoverished conception of the national culture also underpins the Hillgate Group's (1987) critique of anti-racist and multicultural education. From an unequivocal assimilationist stance, the group disparages those teachers 'who desire to lock ethnic minorities within their own languages and customs and to isolate them from the greater society of which they are a part'. It urges the government 'to treat the Swann Report with the scepticism it deserves'. According to the group, Swann 'engages our post-colonial guilt feelings' and 'threatens to destroy the basis of our national culture' (Hillgate Group 1987:3–4). This statement, as Jack Demaine (1988:253) has pointed out, is reminiscent of Mrs Thatcher's 'infamous reference' in 1978 to the fear of 'being swamped by people of a different culture'.

Despite the ethnocentricism and seemingly strident nation-alism of New Right ideologues, most (as we show in Chapter 3) would deny that their standpoint was in any way racist. As Randall has argued:

> The majority . . . do not wish to claim any genetically endowed superiority over other races [*sic*] and cultures. They state simply that people have a cultural preference for those who share that culture: they only wish to maintain their own, unsullied by proximity to others! This, they insist, is a 'natural' inclination and moral juridical right.
>
> (Randall 1988:4)

As we have already indicated, those on the Right also attempt to discredit and marginalize anti-racism by denying the nature and extent of racism in the UK. The New Right's commitment to deracialized policies in education stems (in part) from the belief that the UK is an essentially 'tolerant' society and that racism is confined to an aberrant minority. For many years now, the UK's Afro-Caribbean and South Asian communities have repudiated this 'rotten apple theory of racism' by highlighting the existence and prevalence of 'institutional racism' in educa-tion (and in other spheres), and by drawing attention to the full impact of racial harassment and violence on the lives of black people. The anti-racist movement in education developed in response to increasing concern about these issues in the 1970s and to 'grassroots' demands for policies to promote racial justice and equality both in schools and society at large. Let us deal first with the issue of racial violence, focusing on the symbolic significance of the murders of Gurdip Singh Chaggar in 1976 and of Altab Ali in 1978.

'Blood on the Streets'

On 3 June 1976, a report appeared in *The Times* which drew attention to mounting disquiet within the UK's South Asian population. It noted that the atmosphere had been soured by organizations such as the National Front, 'which have taken out provocative processions through immigrant areas'. The report went on to state that 'attacks on immigrant-owned businesses and innocent people have not been uncommon'. The following day, Gurdip Singh Chaggar was attacked and murdered by five youths outside a public house in Southall, London. Angry demonstrations followed, as a collective wave of anger swept South Asian youngsters on to the streets. The death of Chaggar, according to Tuku Mukherjee,

> was not only a great tragedy for all those who knew him, but it also brought home to anyone in the community the brutal reality of racism, and the futility of hoping that 'time' or 'reason' would diminish its effects.
>
> (Mukherjee 1988:220)

Although the murder was to trigger a wide-ranging debate about the state of 'race' relations in the UK, the initial response of the government was to play down its significance. For example, Mr Brynmor John (then Minister of State at the Home Office) described the incident as 'just a hiccup', before going on to castigate Enoch Powell for 'having made speeches over the past eight years damaging to race relations' (*Guardian*, 9 June 1976). Speaking about Chaggar's murder in the Commons, the Prime Minister, James Callaghan, urged the public 'not to allow passion to destroy Britain's reputation as a tolerant, cohesive and unified society' (*The Times*, 9 June 1976).

Other commentators, however, did not endorse Callaghan's sanguine view of the situation. For example, Dr Coggan, the Archbishop of Canterbury, who was speaking at a press conference to launch his book *Dear Archbishop*, roundly condemned racist attacks as 'shameful', and 'provocative race marches as doing incalculable harm to community relations' (*Guardian*, 15 June 1976). In the ensuing debate, the primate's comments were to evoke a hostile response from sections of the media. A *Telegraph* leader informed its readers:

> Dr Coggan seems wholly to have missed the point. If we're looking for scapegoats, then they are to be found among failed urban programmes, immigrant schools without English teachers, inefficient housing programmes, as well as among National Front demonstrators. . . . It would have

benefited Dr Coggan's vocation to show at least some
sympathy for those who feel their own *national way of life* is
menaced by this sudden and massive infusion of *alien* culture.

(Telegraph, 16 June 1976; emphasis added)

John Turner, writing in the *Sunday Express*, continued the
attack on what he referred to as 'Dr Coggan's sanctimonious
spiel'. Turner opined that 'there was not a single word of
compassion for working-class white people, who have seen
areas in which they were born and brought up turn before their
eyes into coloured ghettos'. He concluded with the following
allusion to 'Britain's reputation as a tolerant, cohesive and
unified society':

> People in this country are not and never have been racialists,
> but have been driven to desperation because of idiots of
> politicians who even now put a smokescreen round the truth
> about the continuing flood of immigration.
>
> *(Sunday Express*, 20 June 1976)

In view of such sentiments, it is not surprising that leaders of
the South Asian communities called upon the government to
issue a statement to the effect that 'Britain intends to preserve
its multiracial, multicultural society'. They also demanded an
official inquiry into the causes of racial tension and violence
(*The Times*, 23 June 1976). The government, however, did not
succumb to these pressures, despite the observation that: 'the
worsening of race relations in the United Kingdom has given
members of the Asian community considerable cause for alarm
and concern, which has become more intense in the past few
months' (*The Times*, 22 June 1976).

The violence and harassment, which continued throughout
the long, hot summer of 1976, served to stimulate the development of a 'grassroots' resistance movement. In East London the
Anti-racist Committee of Asians organized a protest march
from Brick Lane to Leman Street Police Station in support of its
demand for 'effective and impartial action by the police and
authorities against racist attacks and provocation' (Bethnal
Green and Stepney Trades Council 1978:55). In the autumn of
1976, Rock Against Racism (RAR) was established to counter

the growing influence on young people of neo-fascist organizations, such as the National Front. Employing a formula which has subsequently been emulated by Live Aid, Band Aid and other progressive initiatives, RAR 'used music to get conventional antiracist ideas across to a pop audience' (Widgery 1986:115). Although RAR attracted many established performers, in David Widgery's view it was essentially a grass-roots movement 'not started by university graduates, but by cultural autodidacts working in photography, the glossies, theatre, rock and roll, graphic design and fashion' (Widgery 1986:54).

Two years after Chaggar's death, another tragedy gave further impetus to the development of anti-racist initiatives. On 4 May 1978, a 25-year-old clothing machinist, Altab Ali, was stabbed to death in Whitechapel, on his way home from work. The murder was racially motivated, as Widgery explains:

> Altab Ali's killers were teenage boys: Roy Arnold, aged seventeen, of Limehouse, Carl Ludlow, aged seventeen, of Bow, and an unnamed mixed-race boy from Poplar, aged sixteen. It was the sixteen-year-old who did the stabbing and when the police asked him why, his chilling reply was 'For no reason at all'. He stated, as if it were commonplace, 'If we saw a Paki we used to have a go at them. We would ask for money and beat them up. I've beaten up Pakis on at least five occasions.' To these boys, simply by being Asian, Altab Ali was a potential target. For one, the killing of another black was a kind of initiation ceremony, his ticket of admission into white male society.
>
> (Widgery 1986:16)

On 14 May, following Ali's funeral, more than 7,000 people, mostly Bengalis, marched from Whitechapel to a protest rally in Hyde Park. It was described at the time 'as one of the biggest demonstrations by Asians ever seen in Britain'. The demonstrators shouted: ' "Law and order for whom?"; "Self defence is no offence"; "Black and white unite and fight"; "Who killed Altab Ali? Racism, racism." ' (Bethnal Green and Stepney Trades Council 1978:56).

The Trades Council's report, *Blood on the Streets*, showed

that the attack on Ali was by no means an isolated incident in this part of London. On the contrary, 'the barrage of harassment, insult and intimidation, week in week out, fundamentally determines how the immigrant community here lives and works' and 'how the host community and the authorities are viewed'. (Bethnal Green and Stepney Trades Council 1978:3). Such was the level of mistrust between the Bengalis and the police that few racial incidents were reported. Victims were even sceptical about describing their experiences to the researchers. Thirty-six 'serious incidents' were recorded during the first eight months of 1978. Arguably the most brazen occurred on 11 June, when about 200 white youths rampaged in Brick Lane, smashing windows (Bethnal Green and Stepney Trades Council 1978:80).

In an attempt to stem the rising tide of racism, both in the capital and elsewhere in the country, the Anti-Nazi League (ANL) was established in 1977. In common with other anti-racist organizations, this alliance was broadly based and was sponsored by various 'big names' from politics, the arts, sport and popular entertainment, including Neil Kinnock, David Edgar, Brian Clough and Miriam Karlin. 'To make politics more fun and music more political', the ANL and RAR jointly organized a political rally in Trafalgar Square and an open-air concert in Victoria Park, East London on 30 April 1978. An estimated 100,000 demonstrators participated in the rally. As Widgery recounts:

> By midday the whole lot were there – Old Left, New Left and Left Out, punks and hippies and skins, vicars and trade unionists, blacks, browns and pinks. It was certainly the biggest anti-fascist rally since the thirties.
>
> (Widgery 1986:85)

Commentating on the impact of this and similar events, he goes on to claim: 'If such a campaign had not been launched in Britain, then there is every reason to suspect that the mid-1970s' electoral surge of the NF might have been sustained' (Widgery 1986:111).

The ANL spawned many sub-groups in the late-1970s, including Teachers Against the Nazis (TAN) and All London

Teachers Against Racism and Fascism (ALTARF). Their members were to be at the forefront of the campaign for anti-racist education. ALTARF, for example, was formed in 1978, with the declared aim of challenging racism both in schools and out. As a result of pressures emananting from this organization (and others), many schools were to formulate their own anti-racist policies, often well in advance of any concerted action which was taken by the local authority (see Troyna and Williams 1986:67).

ALTARF noted, in the conclusion to its policy document, *Racism in Schools* (1979), that 'the structure, organisation and day to day workings of the school can be racist, intentionally or unintentionally'. Sensitive to growing anxieties among Afro-Caribbeans about various facets of educational provision, ALTARF urged teachers 'to monitor suspension, ESN school placement, the nature and effect of streaming and banding, and to examine this in the context of racism overall' (ALTARF 1979:22). We shall now trace the development of these anxieties.

The ESN issue: a symbol of black 'underachievement'

Disquiet within the Afro-Caribbean community about institutionalized inequality in education can be traced back to the mid-1960s, when the North London West Indian Association (NLWIA) began its campaign in the London Borough of Haringey against the high number of black referrals to schools for the educationally sub-normal (ESN). At that time, the population of Afro-Caribbean pupils in the borough's ESN schools was in the region of 70 per cent (Hassan and Beese 1981). Concern about the invidious position of Afro-Caribbeans in education was not simply confined to Haringey. A survey published by the Inner London Education Authority (ILEA) in 1967 not only indicated that black pupils were over-represented in ESN schools but also revealed that many teachers who worked in this sector of education believed that this over-representation arose because many of the children were often wrongly classified. These teachers, as Sally Tomlinson has noted, believed that 'a misplacement was four times as likely in the case of immigrant children and that the methods and processes of assessment were the major reasons for this misplacement' (S. Tomlinson 1981:75).

The campaign gained further momentum in 1971 with the publication of Bernard Coard's pamphlet, *How the West Indian Child is Made Educationally Sub-normal in the British School System*. Coard maintained that, as a result of culturally biased and inaccurate testing procedures and of low teacher expectations, black children were more likely to be labelled as 'slow learners' or 'difficult' and then consigned to the lower streams in secondary schools or schools for the educationally subnormal. We consider Coard's critique in more detail in Chapter 2. Here we want to point out that over 10,000 copies of the pamphlet were sold and this not only reflected the extent of concern but also helped to ensure that the ESN issue remained on the agenda throughout the 1970s. Despite this concern, the DES continued to resist pressures to implement specific measures to obviate racial inequality in schools, at least until 1979. Then Shirley Williams, the Secretary of State for Education, set up the Committee of Inquiry into the Education of Children from Ethnic Minority Groups, with Anthony Rampton in the chair. The committee was given the following brief: 'to review the educational needs and attainments of children from ethnic minority groups, giving early and particular attention to the educational needs and attainments of pupils of West Indian origin' (DES 1981:1). In its interim report, the committee acknowledged the existence of institutional (as well as direct) discrimination in schools, and indicated that this was a factor in disadvantaging black pupils (DES 1981:11–14).

Subsequent inquiries, which were conducted by the Commission for Racial Equality (CRE 1985) and the ILEA (1988), not only lend support to this claim but also suggest that the current anxieties of Afro-Caribbean parents about schooling are not without foundation. The CRE's investigation, which began in 1979, 'arose out of national concern about the number of black pupils who were being suspended from school' (CRE 1985:1). It was undertaken in Birmingham and covered the period 1974–80. The inquiry revealed that black pupils were four times as likely as their white peers to be suspended from secondary school, and more likely to find themselves suspended following a 'direct confrontation' with their teacher. In addition, black pupils had a greater chance of being placed in a suspension unit than pupils from other ethnic backgrounds. The CRE claimed that its evidence 'pointed to institutional, rather than direct or intentional discrimination as the main reason for the differential pattern of treatment' (CRE 1985:2). To substantiate this claim, it showed that teachers' responses towards black pupils were often what David Hargreaves (e.g. 1982) has described as 'deviance provocative': that is, staff tended to adopt a confrontational stance towards this group in the classroom.

This finding serves to reinforce Cecile Wright's (1987) observations about the adverse relationship between many black pupils and their teachers. (We show this in Chapter 2.) Along with other studies (e.g. Mac an Ghaill 1988), the Commission found that staff were less than sympathetic towards Rastafarians whom they perceived as a particular 'threat to their authority and the orderliness of their classrooms' (CRE 1985:33). Affiliation to this sub-culture was found to be 'a significant factor' in the referral of black youngsters to suspension units or educational guidance centres. The Commission concluded its report with the following observation:

> unless careful records are kept and analysed and appropriate action taken, it is easy for discriminatory patterns to develop. In relation to suspension from school and referral to special units, this happened between 1974 and 1980 in Birmingham.
> (Commission for Racial Equality 1985:50)

The ILEA's more recent investigation into suspensions and expulsions also suggests that the disciplinary procedures that are adopted by schools may discriminate against black pupils (ILEA 1988). Focusing on the academic year 1986–7, the study revealed that 'in both primary and secondary schools pupils from a Caribbean background were over-represented amongst those suspended and expelled from school and pupils from Asian and White European backgrounds were under-represented' (ILEA 1988:14). Whereas 'Caribbean' boys formed only 13.3 per cent of the secondary school population, they accounted for 34.5

per cent of the total suspensions; the corresponding figures given for white boys were 65.0 per cent and 51.2 per cent respectively (ILEA 1988:17). Although the data relating to girls showed a similar pattern, the overall proportion of girls who were suspended was much lower than that of boys. The reasons which were provided by headteachers for suspending pupils were also analysed in terms of gender and ethnic differences. The ILEA found:

> With the boys, over 50 per cent of those from a Caribbean background were suspended for a 'single severe incident', whereas of those from a White European background the corresponding proportion was only 42 per cent. . . . With the girls, a higher proportion (74% v. 54%) of those from a Caribbean background, compared to those from a White European background, were suspended for a 'single severe incident' or for repeated disruption; by contrast a higher proportion of the White European girls than of the Caribbean girls were suspended for 'other' reasons (46% v. 26%).

> (ILEA 1988:19)

Both the ILEA (1988) and CRE (1985) studies can be criticized for giving undue emphasis to the influence of ethnicity and for failing to take appropriate account of the influence of class. As we show in Chapter 2, the same criticism may also be levelled against many studies of ethnic differences in attainment. Despite the methodological and conceptual weaknesses of the research on suspensions, referrals and explusions, such research (in common with earlier work on Afro-Caribbean placement in ESN schools) does little to disabuse black parents from the belief that the school system is, in some way, 'rigged against' their children. In Chapter 2 we shall look more closely at the evidence for this.

Discussion points

1 What do you see as the main features of 'British culture'? How does your perception differ from John Casey's (1982)?
2 The Hillgate Group has insisted that: 'The deterioration in

British education has arisen partly because schools have been treated as instruments for equalising, rather than instructing, children' (1987). What evidence can you find to support this view?

2 Who gets what?

Introduction

In 1971 the black educationist, activist and politician, Bernard Coard, argued that

> The Black child labours under three crucial handicaps. . . . *Low expectations on his part* about his [*sic*] likely performance in a white-controlled system of education; (2) *Low motivation* to succeed academically because he feels the cards are stacked against him; and finally, (3) *Low teacher expectations* which affect the amount of effort expended on his behalf by the teacher, and also affect his own image of himself and his abilities.
>
> (Coard 1971:25; original emphasis)

As we saw in Chapter 1, this indictment of the UK's education system stemmed from Coard's identification of the disproportionately high number of pupils of Afro-Caribbean origin then assigned to schools for the educationally sub-normal (ESN). His critique centred on the view that many of these pupils had been misclassified as ESN, the reason being that the system was 'rigged' against them. Coard, suggested that these issues could be resolved in two ways. First, steps would need to be taken to increase parental participation in education. Second, it was essential to set up community-sponsored schools. Coard insisted:

> Through these schools, we hope to make up for the inadequacies of the British school system, and for its refusal to teach our children our history and our culture. We must never sit idly by while they make ignoramuses of our

children, but must see to it that by hook or crook our children
get the best education they are capable of!

(Coard: 1971:39)

Fully fifteen years after the publication of Coard's pamphlet,
there appeared three reports into education provision in multi-
ethnic areas of London. The first of these was a study of
secondary education in Brent, headed by Jocelyn Barrow.
Amongst other things, her research team reported how black
parents, and especially those of Afro-Caribbean background,
tended to view schools primarily in terms of their 'instrumental'
role. These parents perceived the school as 'an instrument of
liberation', to use the research team's phrase, and expected it to
play an important role in furthering the life-chances of their
children. But these expectations were unfulfilled. According to
Barrow and her colleagues, these same parents were 'shocked' in
finding that 'the school in which they have invested so much
hope and faith seems to fail their children' (Barrow *et al.*
1986:474): A couple of years later HMI came to the same
conclusions: 'parents from Caribbean backgrounds' in Brent
were, exceptionally, 'unsupportive of the schools that their
children attended' (HMI 1987:para. 39). A similar picture
emerges in the London Borough of Hackney. There a team of
consultants reported 'very deep concern about the education of
black and ethnic minority children among the communities' and
'a deep-rooted mistrust of the system' (Focus 1988:13).

What is going on? After all, looking back on the period
separating the publication of Coard's pamphlet from the reports
on Brent and Hackney, we see that this comprised the liberal
moment in the politics of racial equality in the UK. These years
witnessed the emergence of a powerful rhetoric on multiculturalism and, in the more recent past, anti-racist conceptions of
reform. Needless to say, the achievements of this period in
expediting racial equality were less than the rhetoric would have
us believe. In education, for instance, the flurry of activity
tended to be confined to those local education authorities and
their individual schools which served ethnically mixed communities. None the less, during these years, multicultural (and in
some areas, anti-racist) education concerns found their way on

to the policy-making agenda. What is m
number of these policies and associated prac
towards enhancing the academic performanc
especially those of Afro-Caribbean origin, a
precisely the effects of misclassification to whic
had drawn attention. In this sense, therefore
imated to the form of multiculturalism that ....cu by
Margaret Gibson as 'Benevolent Multiculturalism':

> The conditions giving rise to this approach are, first, the
> continuing academic failure of students from a certain minor-
> ity ethnic group whose school performance continues to lag
> behind national norms, and second, the rejection of cultural
> and genetic deficit hypotheses regarding students' school
> failure.
>
> (Gibson 1976:7)

Despite these initiatives, the picture remains remarkably stable.
Distrust and disenchantment continue to typify black parents'
views of the British school system. Indeed, if we are to accept
the validity of the data that were collected from five LEAs by
Lord Swann and his colleagues (DES 1985a), along with those
that were assembled by the Research and Statistics (R and S)
branch of the ILEA (1987), then it seems that children of Afro-
Caribbean parents continue to perform less well in examinations than most of their classmates of South Asian or white
indigenous backgrounds. Of course, as we shall see later, caveats
have been expressed about the use of public examinations as a
valid index of attainment. We will also be introduced to the
long-standing and vigorous debate about the relative power of
'race', class, gender and school as predictors of academic
performance. We are not going to deny the veracity or perti-
nence of these concerns. At the same time, it is impossible to
turn a blind eye to differential patterns of performance along
ethnic lines and their apparent resilience or, most importantly,
to underestimate their impact on the way in which parents of
Afro-Caribbean origin, in particular, view the educational
system.

Gutmann, in her espousal of 'nonrepression' as an underpinning principle of education, argues that: 'For an educational system to be democratic, all children must be educated to participate intelligently in the politics that shape their society' (Gutmann 1988:186). We agree. Our commitment to a broadly conceived interpretation of anti-racist education derives from a similar conviction that all pupils must be incorporated in the development of more emancipatory forms of education. Involvement cannot and should not be contingent on spatial, residential or demographic factors. In simple terms this means that 'all-white' schools, alongside those serving multi-ethnic communities, should be implicated in the move towards anti-racist education. Following the Australian sociologist, Lyn Yates (1988), whose work has focused on the development of strategies to combat sexism in education, we see the struggle for anti-racism as crystallizing around two distinctive but related aspects of schooling. The first of these deals with 'who gets what' and demands attention to the formal criteria that are used for the distribution of scarce educational rewards and the characteristics of their recipients. 'Who gets what', or selection, relates directly to one of the most fundamental roles of education: the differentiation, classification and certification of pupils through explicit and generally accepted criteria. As we have seen, concern with who gets what figures prominently in the way in which black parents perceive and evaluate the educational system.

'Learning' is the other aspect of schooling that is highlighted by Yates. By this she means 'what students learn about themselves and the world' during their school experiences. By definition this consists of a more diffuse, informal and less ordered range of issues. It impels discussion of what is often termed the hidden curriculum: that is, school administrative and organizational arrangements and practices, and social relationships. Together, these comprise the prevailing ethos and *modus operandi* of the institution.

'Selection' and 'learning' are therefore useful analytical tools in deconstructing and identifying the various ways in which racism (and the practices to which it gives rise) operates in a range of educational settings, be they multi-ethnic or 'all-white' (Troyna 1989). However, it is important to recognize that their separation is for analytical purposes only and that, in reality, they are mutually reinforcing in the maintenance and reproduction of inequality. In this chapter we shall be looking at their operation in multi-ethnic schools, focusing primarily on who gets what and why. In Chapter 3 we shall address more directly the issue of racism amongst white pupils and how this contributes to the oppression of black people in the UK.

Who gets what?

The way in which schools are organized in the UK legitimates a competitive system in which prestigious educational rewards are scarce. Thus, there are, and will remain, few winners and many losers. What continues to tantalize are the criteria that are used in determining how the selection procedure and certification process operate in schools. Ostensibly, the *formal* criteria derive from the idea of meritocracy, a principle enshrined in the 1944 Education Act. Accordingly, individual talent, as measured by public examinations, rather than ascriptive criteria (such as class, gender or 'race') was sanctioned as the pre-eminent criterion in deciding 'who gets what'. According to this view, the educational system assumes the role of a neutral allocator and regulator of credentials: class-blind, gender-blind and 'race' blind, but talent-friendly! Indeed, since 1944 a key role for state education has been to organize and secure public consent for meritocratic principles. It is here that the phrase, equality of opportunity, has assumed such symbolic importance; it encapsulates and expresses succinctly the essence of the meritocratic ideal. In the event, however, it has flattered to deceive. It sits uneasily alongside a range of empirical research which has uncovered a tenacious pattern of class, gender and racial inequality in the educational opportunities that are available, the courses that are followed and the qualifications that are obtained (see Burgess 1986:73–127). Let us be clear about these trends. They are neither arbitrary nor subject to dramatic fluctuation and change. They are persistent, some might say institutionalized, inequalities which are neither accidental nor incidental. Informal criteria, we shall soon see, play an influential and systematic part in decisions about 'who gets what' and the distribution of future life-chances.

Of course, underpinning the belief that it is worthwhile to attend school for a minimum of 15,000 hours is the assumption that the credentials that it has to offer provide access to the labour market. As a derivative of the principle of equality of opportunity, this remains a seductive and plausible proposition: doing well at school guarantees success in the labour market. This is the essence of the unwritten contract between state and individual: compulsory attendance at school from the ages of 5–16 in return for a position in the labour market which is commensurate with the talent that is demonstrated, and re-warded accordingly, at school. Needless to say, this 'tightening bond' thesis linking educational credentials to position in the labour market has never been as clear cut as conventional wisdom would have us believe. On the one hand, the economic recession and its specified impact on young school-leavers has thrown into sharp relief the tenuous relationship between educational and occupational status. On the other, the differential experiences of female and male, black and white youngsters in their search for a job has highlighted the important part that is played by employers' discretionary judgements and informal, covert practices and assumptions in the transition from education/training spheres to the labour market. We will return to this point later in the chapter.

Equality of opportunity in education thus has a serious credibility problem. However, it would be wrong to infer a general disavowal by black parents of the meritocracy as an ideal from the evidence of their dissatisfaction with the way in which schools are presently constituted. On the contrary, as Barrow's report on Brent revealed in 1986, Afro-Caribbean parents, in particular, endorse this conception of education. Similarly, the rise of the black voluntary school movement and its emphasis on the teaching of basic skills (Chevannes and Reeves 1987) and the provisional support for a national curriculum that is offered by black parents in Hackney (Focus 1988) demonstrate a commitment to strategies and procedures which offer some assurance that meritocratic principles, above all else, determine 'who gets what'.

When we designate a group of pupils as 'underachievers' we can mean one of two things. We might be referring to the fact that the group is performing less well than would have been predicted on the basis of standardized tests of ability. In this case it could be owing to the fact that the *potential performance* of the group is less than might have been expected by the test. Alternatively, underachievement might refer to the lower mean attainment of a group of pupils in comparison with the mean attainment of another group; for instance, comparing the relative mean attainment of working-class and middle-class pupils, of girls and boys, or of Afro-Caribbean and white European pupils. However, if this comparative analysis is to have any meaning or relevance it must be assumed that 'the same distribution of ability and aptitude' obtains for both groups (Jeffcoate 1982:15). Implicitly, if not explicitly, therefore, this second mode of analysis discounts the possibility that the 'underachieving' group has an innately lower intellect than the group(s) to which it is being compared. Studies of the academic performance of pupils of Afro-Caribbean origin tend to be based on inter-group comparisons. Therefore, when these pupils are typified as 'underachievers' this is in relation to pupils from other ethnic group backgrounds (Troyna 1984a). Consider, for instance, Bhikku Parekh's comments on the ILEA's ethnically based statistics of the 'O' level and CSE examination results for 1985 and 1986:

> the percentage of Afro-Caribbean children failing to take O and CSE level examinations has steadily increased since 1976. At the same time the number of those securing five or more higher grades has also increased from just under 2 per cent in 1976 to well over 4 per cent in 1985 and 1986. *While this is encouraging, it is still only half as good as the whites, and just over one sixth as good as the Indian.*
>
> (Parekh 1987:26; emphasis added)

Now, if inter-group comparisons are used to establish whether or not pupils of Afro-Caribbean origin are 'underachieving', was it not irrelevant, even racist, for Lord Swann and his colleagues to commission a research paper on the possible relationship between IQ and 'West Indian underachievement' in their report, *Education for All* (DES 1985a)? The confusion surrounding the issue of 'black underachievement', which Lord Swann and his colleagues hoped to clarify (but in effect compounded), has characterized this debate since it first hit the headlines in the late 1960s. In 1975, Alan Little and his colleagues in the ILEA reported that the relatively poorer performance of Afro-Caribbean pupils stretched across all areas of the curriculum: passive and active vocabulary, verbal reasoning, reading, English, mathematics and study skills (Little 1975). However, this was conceived as a transitory problem. In accordance with the *zeitgeist* on race-related issues, progressive liberals opined that these differences would diminish with the passage of time once 'strangeness' had become 'familiar'. This commitment to the 'contact hypothesis' as the ubiquitous panacea for race-related problems was misplaced, however. As we have already indicated, the 'underachievement' of black British pupils has endured as a permanent feature of the educational landscape.

By the mid-1970s, concern with the relatively poorer academic performance of these pupils extended well beyond the confines of educational settings. Indeed, even in 1969, the Select Committee on Race Relations and Immigration (SCRRI) had warned of the dangers of denying these youngsters equality of opportunity in education. It was here that the 'seeds of racial discord' would be sown, according to the SCRRI (1969:6–7). The 'black explosion' in British schools and their neighbourhoods, which was documented by Faroukh Dhondy and colleagues in the *Race Today* collective, did little to assuage anxieties (Dhondy *et al.* 1982). 'The relative underachievement of West Indian pupils', noted the SCRRI in its 1977 report, 'seriously affects their future employment prospects and is a matter of major importance both in education terms and *in the context of race relations*' (SCRRI 1977:xx; emphasis added). By the time disturbances erupted on the streets of Bristol in 1980, in Brixton, Toxteth and Moss Side in 1981, and, four years later, in Tottenham and Handsworth, many others had come round to this way of thinking. 'The real causes of the trouble', suggested Lord Scarman after the 1985 disturbances, 'are bad housing, jobs and education. Education above all' (*Sunday Times*, 12 January 1986). Lord Swann and his committee, in a government-sponsored investigation into the education of children from ethnic minority groups, followed the same line of argument. Their data on the differential examination performance of school-leavers from different ethnic origins confirmed the findings of the committee's 1981 interim report: children of Afro-Caribbean origin were performing less well than pupils from other ethnic backgrounds. The committee recognized that this spelt danger and that the imperative was to formulate an educational orthodoxy that might pre-empt 'the fragmentation of our society along ethnic lines'. Such a possibility would, in the committee's view, 'threaten the stability and cohesion of society as a whole' (DES 1985a:7)

The enduring (and seemingly immutable) pattern of 'under-achievement', with its causal link to the cohesion and stability, or otherwise, of society, strengthened rather than weakened the state's commitment to the notion of a meritocracy. In other words, the liberal premises of a meritocracy were perceived as inviolable and sacrosanct; what required attention was its application. In this context it is not surprising that the years immediately following the urban disorders witnessed the emergence of a range of reformist practices and procedures which was designed ostensibly to deal with the technical malfunctioning of the meritocratic system and to enhance the educational performance of Afro-Caribbean pupils. As Troyna argued in 1984: 'the fear has been another "explosion", the solution: enhance the academic performance of black youth, the means: multicultural education' (Troyna 1984b:80). Such developments were not without precedent. In the USA, for instance, the race-related urban disorders of the 1960s were also followed swiftly by a knee-jerk response from the state: namely, the sponsorship of various multicultural education programmes. The intention was to restore the black community's faith in the legitimacy of schooling as a neutral provider of opportunities for mobility.

We have seen that when the relatively poor performance of pupils of Afro-Caribbean background first came to light, it was viewed by educationists and policy-makers as a function of the cultural distance between the school and the child's home environment. During the 1970s, the contact hypothesis, which embraced both the 'explanation' and 'solution' was eschewed in favour of a more radical diagnosis. This stated that the school and the curriculum that it legitimated was blatantly antagonistic to the culture of black children. It undermined their confidence, inhibited their motivation to succeed and depressed their academic performance. As the 1990s get underway , however, we can see that this interpretation of 'underachievement', which gave rise to multicultural education, remains under critical scrutiny. After all, despite the proliferation of multicultural education initiatives, the pattern of 'who gets what' has hardly altered. The question is why?

What is going on?

Writing in 1983, Bhikhu Parekh claimed that the debate about black underachievement 'is vitiated by what I might call the fallacy of the single factor' (Parekh 1983:113). Reductionist interpretations of underachievement are, of course, signalled by the confidence that is invested in the contact hypothesis and in multicultural education as viable solutions. Jenny Williams has developed this further and shown that the diagnoses of working-class underachievement in the 1960s and the under-achievement of black pupils crystallize around four discernible and (whilst in the ascendancy) definitive paradigms: cultural deficit, cultural difference, teacher stereotyping and labelling, and discrimination within an unequal structure of opportunities (J. Williams 1986:143). Perhaps, however, the fallacy of the single factor' arises from an inadequate conceptualization of the issue? Let us see.

In some of our other work (e.g. Carrington and Short 1989; Troyna 1984a; 1986; 1988), we have suggested that the debate about 'black underachievement' has suffered from the failure to specify the *explanandum*; that is, the phenomenon to be explained. Are we sure, for instance, that it is Afro-Caribbean pupils *per se* who are 'underachieving' and who constitute the phenomenon that we need to address? The answer is no. What we are sure of is that, when ethnicity is privileged as an organizing category in analyses of 'who gets what', it is those pupils whose ethnicity is defined as Afro-Caribbean who perform relatively badly. Ethnicity is therefore ascribed with explanatory status, as witnessed in the interim and final reports of the committee of inquiry into the education of children from ethnic minority groups (DES 1981; 1985a; see Table 2.1).

Thus, in attempting to explain the differential academic performance of pupils of Afro-Caribbean and South Asian origin, Lord Swann and his colleagues invoked a range of empirically spurious but none the less popular stereotypes which were attributed to these ethnic groups. 'Asians', we are told, are given to

'keeping their heads down' and 'adopting a low profile' thereby making it easier to succeed in a hostile environment. West Indians, by contrast, are given to 'protest' and 'a high profile' with the reverse effect.

(DES 1985a:86)

In the effort to attribute causal status to ethnicity, in the examination of 'who gets what', we can see how these racist depictions of 'Asians' and 'West Indians' might arise. However, the ethnic paradigm, of which the Swann report is a classic exemplar, begs a number of questions. First, is it legitimate to define 'Afro-Caribbean' as an ethnic group? As Ellis Cashmore informs us, an ethnic group 'is not a mere aggregate of people or a sector of a population, but a *self-conscious* collection of people united, or closely connected, by shared experiences' (Cashmore 1988:97; emphasis added). The evidence at hand suggests that not all young people whose familial origins are to be found in the Caribbean would wish to define themselves primarily in these terms (Mac an Ghaill 1988; Troyna 1979). Second, on what social scientific grounds should ethnicity be privileged over, say, class, gender, age, geographical location or type of school attended as the interpretative framework in which the analysis of 'who gets what' takes place? After all, research tells us that each of these variables is causally linked, to a greater or lesser degree, to academic performance. Third, to what extent might the limitations of ethnicity as an analytical categorization

Table 2.1 'O' Level and CSE achievement (in percentages)

	Asians		West Indians		All other leavers		Total school leavers from five LEAs		All maintained school leavers in England	
	1978/79	1981/82	1978/79	1981/82	1978/79	1981/82	1978/79	1981/82	1978/79	1981/82
No graded results (including those who attempted no examinations)	20	19	17	19	22	19	21	19	14	11
At least 1 graded result but less than 5 higher graded results	63	64	80	75	62	62	64	63	66	66
5 or more higher graded results	17	17	3	6	16	19	15	18	21	23
Total leavers (number)	466	571	718	653	5,012	4,718	6,196	5,942	693,840	706,690

Source: DES 1985a:114

be mitigated by its disaggregation into more meaningful and nuanced groups? In short, should we not be analysing the *interaction* of variables, such as ethnicity, gender and class, in the production of school performance rather than isolating them into discrete, independent units? By ignoring the interactive relationship of these variables, we are conflating a diverse, complex and (potentially) contradictory series of experiences into a single, undifferentiated category: ethnicity.

In posing these questions we are not denying that the data, as presently constituted, point to the comparatively lower mean attainment of Afro-Caribbean pupils in public examinations. However, we also know from the research of Barbara Tizard and her colleagues that, on entry to infant school, black and white children start from 'essentially the same academic position' (Tizard *et al.* 1988:109). Alongside Peter Mortimore's finding that, even after adjustments are made for other significant background factors, black children, including those of South Asian and Afro-Caribbean origin, make poorer progress than white children in reading during their junior school (Mortimore *et al.* 1988:152–3), it suggests that focusing on the observable outcomes of 15,000 hours of schooling (i.e. performance in 16+ examinations) is simply insufficient ground on which to base analyses. To explore who gets what (and why), we need to examine what goes on in school regarding the various processes of classification and differentiation of pupils. It would seem from Mortimore's research, in particular, that these processes help to define and confine pupils' experiences of education and, perhaps, their life in general. The processes constitute part of what pupils learn about themselves as individuals and as members of a group which is evaluated in racist terms. Having said this, more recent research in the area of 'school effectiveness' has suggested that, when appropriate account is taken of social background, school ethos and other relevant variables, the effect of ethnic background on pupil progress is minimized (Smith and Tomlinson 1989). Let us explore this a little more closely.

The 'racial frame of reference'

In our view, the research of Richard Jenkins (1986) into the selection criteria that are used by managers in the recruitment of labour into manual and non-manual occupations provides a useful starting-point for exploring the internal processes of selection and differentiation within schools. In 1980–3, Jenkins interviewed 172 managers from 40 work organizations in the manufacturing, retailing and public sectors in the West Midlands region. His aim was to identify factors which serve to limit black workers' access to jobs. He found that the basis for managerial decision-making in recruitment derived from two broad categories of selection criteria. 'Suitability', according to Jenkins, refers to criteria which are functionally specific; that is, the extent to which the applicants' formal qualifications and training prepare them to perform the tasks of the job competently. 'Acceptability', on the other hand, denotes a range of functionally non-specific criteria. These relate to the applicants' characteristics, which are more diffuse, less easy to specify and codify. Ultimately, they relate to how far the manager reckons that the applicant would 'fit in' to the ethos and practices of the organization. Jenkins concluded from his research that acceptability criteria included both idiosyncratic and ethnocentric components. The former were highly variable; the latter were 'held in common by managers from a common cultural background and rooted in that taken-for-granted frame of reference' (Jenkins 1986:77). Jenkins found that 'in some senses' acceptability criteria were preeminent in determining labour market outcomes (1986:50). Put another way, the intuition, gut-feeling, or 'professional judgement' of managers, which was sometimes predicated on racist and other culturally loaded perceptions of an applicant's ability, manageability or appropriateness, often played a major part in the allocation of the jobs. 'Acceptability' criteria, which tended to be informal, implicit and (often) unaccountable, provided the opportunity for racist assumptions and perceptions to flourish, almost with impunity. As Jenkins points out, racist interpretations of an applicant's 'acceptability' within the organization may not be in the forefront of the manager's mind in making a decision; none the less,

The ethnocentrism of many of the components of acceptability is of relevance to the discussion of *indirect* discrimination. None of these criteria are [*sic*] necessarily racially prejudiced, nor do they involve the *intent* to discriminate against black workers, for whatever reason. In their unintended consequences, however, there is good reason to suppose that they will systematically place mainly black job seekers at a disadvantage.

(Jenkins 1986:77)

This analysis is fully compatible with the research in education that has looked at the way in which decisions about black pupils are both reached and legitimated. On the whole, decisions tend to be premised on ethnocentric assumptions about how best black pupils might 'fit in' to the educational system. Troyna and Williams (1986), for instance, have argued that, in the 1960s and 1970s, a process of 'discrimination by proxy' took place precisely because policy-makers and practitioners operated with acceptability criteria which, although not intentionally discriminatory, none the less derived from a taken-for-granted expectation of the position and status of black pupils and their cultures in the society. Thus, cultural and language differences were defined in deficit terms; the contact hypothesis was put into operation in a way which ensured that only black pupils were dispersed through the system of bussing; and routinized assumptions about school meals, assemblies and clothing were seen as sacrosanct. In addition, these assumptions were also sanctioned by entrenched professional views about what constitutes good practice. Troyna and Ball, in a 1985 study of how schools responded to their LEA's policy on multicultural education, found that resistance was often expressed through teachers' tenacious commitment to the principles of universalism and individualism. Assertions such as 'we treat them all the same' (colour blind) and 'we respond to the *individual* needs of our children' (child-centred) constitute professional tenets which are incompatible with policies that are designed to address the needs and interests of an entire group of pupils, defined in terms of their 'race', gender or class.

The constellation of (acceptability) criteria which serves to underpin professional educationalists' judgements cohere into what Peter Figueroa defines as 'the racial frame of reference'; namely, 'a socially constructed, socially reproduced and the learned way of orienting with and towards others and the world' (Figueroa 1984:19). He goes on to say that the racial frame of reference

> provides those who share it with a rallying point for group loyalty and cohesion. The racial frame of reference helps to bridge the worlds of a socially divided nation and to maintain its national unity against 'outsiders'.
>
> (Figueroa 1984:20)

A review of the research on teachers' racial attitudes suggests that perceptions about black pupils, their respective 'talents' and shortcomings, and their cultural backgrounds are viewed through this lens (Carrington and Short 1989:122–9). The fact that this seems likely to remain part of teachers' ideological baggage for some time to come should also arouse our concern. Research suggests that initial teacher education rarely provides an appropriate context in which this racial frame of reference can be systematically questioned (Cole 1989; Carrington *et al.* 1986; Menter 1987; Tracy, 1986).

Figueroa makes the important point that the racial frame of reference does not simply refer to a set of beliefs but is also informed by and, significantly, informs 'new actions, perception, judgements, thought, knowledge, feeling' and experience (Figueroa 1984:20). Accordingly, it may provide the basis for decision-making: the criteria for differentiation and classification of pupils. This is not to suggest that there is an unequivocable correspondence between attitudes and action; there is not. Measured attitudes are an unreliable predictor of behaviour in many circumstances. However, at the same time, there is evidence that teachers mobilize their 'racial frame of reference' in day-to-day interaction with their pupils. For instance, Cecile Wright, in her ethnographic study of two secondary schools, observed what might best be termed as an adverse relationship between white teachers and pupils of Afro-Caribbean origin. In the researcher's words, the relationship was 'characterized by confrontation and conflict', leading her to believe that school was more of a 'battleground' than a 'learning environment' for these pupils. What interests us in particular is the observable outcome of this social relationship. Wright found that, in decisions about whether Afro-Caribbean pupils should be assigned to CSE or 'O' level examination classes, 'acceptability' overruled suitability criteria. That is to say, the 'acceptability' of such pupils in the higher-status 'O' level classes were perceived and interpreted through their teachers' racial frame of reference. The typification of them as 'discipline problems' overrode a more objective 'suitability' criterion, namely, their performance in the third year 'entry' examination. Consequently, Afro-Caribbean pupils 'more so than any other students' groups, were likely to be placed in ability bands and academic sets well below their actual academic ability' (Wright 1987:123). The analysis in Table 2.2, which is drawn from Wright's study, vividly demonstrates this argument. Wright's study provides a vivid insight into how the racial frame of reference can inform both organizational and classroom practices. Other research lends support to Wright's findings.

During the 1980s we have seen the emergence of a new body of research which has begun to examine, in a systematic and sensitive manner, how the internal processes of schooling impact upon the experiences and life-chances of black pupils. Such research includes Peter Green's (1982) study of the respective nature of classroom interaction between black pupils and teachers, differentiated along an ethnocentric/non-ethnocentric continuum; Sally Tomlinson's (1987) analysis of teachers' decisions about 'appropriate' curriculum option choices for pupils from particular ethnic (and social) groups; and Bruce Carrington's (1983) research on teachers' tendency to view Afro-Caribbean pupils as possessing skills of body rather than skills of mind, and to make decisions accordingly. Although the studies derive from different methodological and disciplinary traditions, they provide an important glimpse into what has been, until recently, 'the black box' of education.

At the very least, this body of new research tells us two things. First, not even the most sophisticated and sensitive analysis of pupils' performance at 16+ examinations can provide

Table 2.2 School B: individual students and allocation to exam sets

Student		Subject marks (out of 100)				Set placement (O = GCE 'O' Level)			
		English	Maths	French	Physics	English	Maths	French	Physics
Afro-Caribbean	A	73	44	58	—	CSE	CSE	CSE	—
	B	62	63	60	59	CSE	CSE	CSE	CSE
	C	64	45	56	72	CSE	CSE	CSE	CSE
	D	68	37	82	—	CSE	CSE	CSE	—
Asian	E	51	77	—	55	O	O	—	O
	F	60	56	58	—	O	O	O	—
	G	61	62	55·5	—	O	O	O	—
	H	54	55	—	40	O	O	—	O
White	I	61	62	—	62	O	O	—	O
	J	52	57	55	—	O	O	O	—
	K	75	82	77·5	72	O	O	O	O
	L	54	75	64	72	O	O	O	O

Source: Wright (1987:124)

anything beyond a limited and partial understanding of who gets what and why. Second, pupils quickly apprehend the way in which teachers see them, their social group and the extent to which they and their group deviate from what Howard Becker defined as the professional conception of the 'ideal pupil' (Becker 1952). In the USA, research has been geared towards assessing, in statistical terms, the extent to which teachers' negative evaluation of black pupils' academic abilities has influenced the latter's motivation to succeed (e.g. Fisher 1981). In the UK, research on this theme has proceeded along qualitative lines (e.g. Mac an Ghaill 1988; Riley 1982). What emerges from these studies, irrespective of their methodology, is that the perception of 'blocked opportunities' (Fisher 1981) circumscribes pupils' commitment to the school, if not to the credentials that it has on offer. In other words, such perceptions influence their view of themselves, of others and of their social world in complex, often negative ways. Against this background it is difficult to dissent from Cecile Wright's claim that: 'the nature of the education experience of black students, especially those of Afro-Caribbean origin, may be better understood in terms of "educational disadvantage" or "inequality" rather than in terms of "underachievement" ' (Wright 1987:126). What do you think?

Discussion points

1 What do you understand by 'the hidden curriculum'? Give examples to show how it may reinforce racial inequality in school.
2 How might schools monitor the effectiveness of an equal opportunities policy? What kinds of data would they need to collect?

3 Racist understanding and understanding racism

'Speaking the unspeakable'

The racial frame of reference, as shown by our analysis of who gets what in education, continues to act as a major constraint on the life-chances of black pupils in the UK. For this reason, we now plan to focus on the issue of racism, especially among children and youth. What exactly is meant by racism, and how do we employ the term in our work? We view racism as a body of ideas which rationalizes and legitimates social practices that reinforce an unequal distribution of power between groups which are distinguished by selected physical and/or cultural characteristics. Along with Bob Carter and Jenny Williams, we would argue that racism refers to an ideological process in which groups of people are held

> to possess certain *unchangeable* characteristics which are constitutive of their 'race'. An attribute (skin colour, religion, country of origin, language) becomes the basis of an individual's identity. It is thus considered to be an unalterable feature of those human beings so defined: for example, greed comes to be regarded as an aspect of 'Jewish-ness', criminality comes to be regarded as an aspect of 'West Indian-ness'.
> Carter and Williams 1987:176–7 emphasis added)

Underlying this process of ascription is the assumption (usually implicit) that the groups so identified are not only mutually exclusive but also either superior or inferior to others. Racism can be manifested in a number of ways. As a feature of everyday thinking (so-called 'commonsense'), it may assume an *individual* form and surface as 'personal prejudice'. However, racism is more than just prejudice. On occasions, racism appears in the form of a 'worked out' *ideology*; that is, a more or less coherent set of beliefs and assumptions about the biological or cultural superiority of certain groups of people. In contrast to the discredited 'scientific racism' of IQ theorists such as William Shockley, Arthur Jensen or Hans Eysenck, most contemporary racist ideologies, as Martin Barker (1981) has argued, eschew 'biologistic' interpretations of social reality. 'The new racism', to use Barker's term, stems from the belief that certain groups of people, usually the national group, have distinctive and inherently superior ways of life, which are threatened by outsiders. In Chapter 1 we provided various examples of this type of thinking when we discussed New Right conceptions of the national culture and characterizations of black people as an 'alien wedge'. Now, in addition to these individual and ideological forms, racism is also expressed *institutionally* 'in the form of systematic practices which deny and exclude blacks from access to social resources' (Wellman 1977: 39). As David Wellman points out, racism can be articulated in both subtle and crude terms, and may be regarded as having both intentional and unintentional forms:

> The essential feature of racism is not hostility or misconception, but rather the defence of a system from which advantage is derived on the basis of race. The manner in which the defence is articulated – either with hostility or subtlety – is not nearly as important as the fact that it insures the continuation of a privileged relationship. Thus, it is necessary to broaden the definition of racism beyond prejudice to include sentiments that, in their consequence if not their intent, support the racial *status quo*.
>
> (Wellman 1977: 221–2).

A cursory examination of the recent evidence on individual racism in the UK suggests that racial attitudes have remained resilient to change, despite legislative, educational and other reforms. This is not to say, however, that there has been no movement in public opinion over the years. Although black people of Afro-Caribbean and South Asian backgrounds continue to face verbal and physical abuse on the streets, at school and in the workplace (CRE 1988; Home Office 1989), such blatant forms of racism are generally perceived by white society as abhorrent and 'beyond the pale'. As Michael Billig and his colleagues (1988) have argued, there has been some perceptible shift in public rhetoric about 'race' and ethnicity since the 1960s. Whereas individual racism continues to be widespread, its more overt manifestations are less likely to meet with public approbation than in the past. Overt racism, because of its associations with the violent extremism of the National Front (NF) or with the bigoted 'bone-headed' view of others on the Far Right, has come to be regarded as lying outside the parameters of respectability. Thus, according to Billig *et al.*, individual racism today tends to be more subtle and often assumes the guise of reasonableness (e.g. 'Blacks are getting more than they deserve'). Contemporary racists, when speaking the unspeakable (that is, making a racist remark), will frequently disavow their own racism by stating: 'I'm not prejudiced, but . . . ' (Billig *et al.* 1988: 106–9).

As we have already noted in our discussion of the 'rotten apple theory of racism', the New Right tends to identify racism with prejudice and to view it as a form of intolerance which is anathema to 'British values and traditions' (whatever these might be). For the New Right, racism (thus conceived) and antiracism are presented as little more than sides of the same coin: both are to be deplored and derided as 'authoritarian', 'subversive' and 'socially divisive'. By defining racism in these restricted terms and, in particular, by ignoring its social and institutional dimension, these critics of anti-racist education seek

> to render the proposition that 'Britain is a racist society' not merely false but meaningless. And thus by rendering the social forms of racism unintelligible, they reduce its explanatory potential. They are able to deny racism as a main factor in racial disadvantage.
>
> (Leicester 1989:10)

Margaret Thatcher's claim that 'people with other faiths and cultures have always been welcomed in our land' and that 'there is no place for racial or religious intolerance in our creed' exemplifies this line of argument (Thatcher 1988). This is true also of Sir Keith Joseph's (1986) rejoinder to the Swann report. He begins by establishing his credentials as a realistic and yet reasonable and tolerant person, writing that 'most prejudice is accompanied by ignorance', and that 'in a free country, people are free to say what they think or feel, within the wide limits set by the law'. Although critical of an assimilationist perspective which demands that 'children from both the majority community and from ethnic minorities should be educated as if ethnic diversity does not exist', he nevertheless goes on to state:

> This position, though unacceptably one-sided, has some elements of good sense. Community by community we have much more in common than dividing us. It would be necessary, therefore, and I believe wrong to turn our education system upside down to accommodate ethnic variety, or to jettison those many features and practices which reflect what is best in our society and its institutions. A British school for British citizens is surely right to transmit to all its pupils a sense of shared national values and traditions.
>
> (Joseph 1986: 201)

From this somewhat toothless attack upon assimilationism, Sir Keith then proceeds to disparage what he sees as another example of 'intolerance': anti-racism. Proponents of this 'extreme' position, he argues, not only 'want to subvert our fundamental values and institutions' but often use the epithet, racist (whether deserved or not), to dismiss those 'who try to apply serious thought and careful argument to the difficult issue of racial prejudice' (Joseph 1986: 202). This is also Ray Honeyford's argument in his recent polemic against those 'who preach and practise the theories of "anti-racism" ': *Integration or Disintegration?* (1988). In common with Sir Keith, Honeyford opens with an unequivocal condemnation of racism as 'an evil thing', arguing that to judge people by the colour of their skin 'is an outrage and that any society that permits this stands condemned by all those with any claim to decent, moral instincts' (1988:ix) Describing his own position as 'non-racist', he repudiates anti-racists for 'creating the a priori assumption that Britain is a racist society' (1988:108) and thereby exaggerating the extent of the problem. According to Honeyford: 'there is little in the survey evidence to support the anti-racist view that Britain is rotted with endemic racism' (1988: 125). The following cameo, based upon his experiences as the headteacher of a Bradford middle school, can be cited as an example of a 'non-racist' position. Honeyford recounts how a 'father of strict Moslem persuasion' arrived at the school and stated that he was not going to allow his daughters to wear uniform. 'They would dress exactly as if they were attending school in Pakistan.' The matter was discussed but not resolved, as Honeyford explains: 'While I felt it important to enable his girls to realise the British side of the cultural identity his decision to raise them in Britain had created, he felt that they must cling to his (but not their) homeland' (1988:254). Honeyford goes on to describe his reaction after the parent had lodged a complaint with the local authority:

> I was informed that the City Council had decided that, if a parent felt more Pakistani than British then he could dress his child in national dress for school. I ruefully conjectured how a headteacher checks just how Pakistani a parent might feel. Perhaps I could adopt the satirist Peter Simple's prejudometer, whereby electrodes are placed on a person's skull and the extent of his prejudice registered on a calibrated dial, or maybe I could use a questionnaire with a five-point Likert scale, varying from passionately to barely Pakistani.
>
> (Honeyford 1988: 255)

Surely, as a result of this encounter, the parent must have left the school with the clear impression that Honeyford not only looked upon his way of life as 'alien' but also regarded his cultural values and traditions with a certain degree of contempt? Whatever his intentions, Honeyford's actions must be judged as racist in their consequences.

In the remainder of this chapter we shall try to support our claims about the resilience of individual racism. Drawing upon a range of quantitative and qualitative studies, we will show that racism is not restricted to any one age group, social class or locality. We will also highlight the early onset of incipient racist attitudes and will explore the views of children and young adults on 'race' and ethnicity. We will give particular attention to the racial attitudes of young white people who live in what Bill Taylor (1986) described as 'non-contact' areas. Having made a case for curricular initiatives to address such attitudes (at both primary and secondary level), we move on to examine in greater detail, the characteristics of 'common-sense' racism, including its idiom, logic and mode of transmission.

Survey evidence: two decades of inertia?

We are not alone in arguing that the questionnaire is a blunt instrument for probing such a sensitive issue as a person's racial attitudes. None the less, surveys provide some indication of prevailing attitudes to 'race' at any given juncture. One of the best known and certainly the most comprehensive survey of 'race' relations in the UK was carried out by E.J.B. Rose and his colleagues for the Institute of Race Relations in 1966–7 (Rose et al. 1969). Working with a sample of 2,250 white adults, who were drawn from five multi-ethnic urban areas, the researchers employed an attitude scale in an attempt to gauge 'the incidence of prejudice'. Of this population, 27 per cent were found to be 'prejudiced' or 'prejudiced inclined', with women tending to be more 'tolerant' than men. However, the finding that only a relatively small proportion of the white population of the UK is 'prejudiced' against black people was to be questioned in subsequent studies (Bagley 1970; Lawrence 1974). It also belied the actual development of political events. As John Rex and Sally Tomlinson have pointed out, at the time of Rose's survey 'electoral opinion was increasingly hostile to black immigration' (Rex and Tomlinson 1979: 238). Enoch Powell's polemical campaign against immigration no doubt contributed to the growth of this hostility. Rose et al.'s sanguine appraisal of 'race' relations in the late 1960s stems, in part, from inadequate conceptualization. By equating personal prejudice with intolerance and hostility, the study is incapable of dealing with the nuances of individual racism. The more subtle, inexplicit, 'respectable' and 'responsible' expressions of individual racism which we referred to earlier would surely have gone unnoticed. The same criticism can also be applied to Adrian Furnham and Barrie Gunter's (1989) contemporary survey of young people's social and political attitudes. Echoing the optimism of Rose and his colleagues, Furnham and Gunter claim that their results should 'bring hope'. They note that, although the majority of their respondents 'did not oppose the view that explicit racial attitudes should be banned' and over a third 'admitted that they were a "little prejudiced" ', the vast majority 'who expressed opinions believed in equality between "races", the use of anti-discrimination legislation, [and] close integration between groups' (Furnham and Gunter 1989: 126). The researchers then draw the following conclusion from their data: 'the majority of young natives [*sic*] are sympathetic to the difficulties of ethnic groups [*sic*] and, for the most part, relatively free of prejudice' (1989: 127). This observation bears little resemblance to the realities of the black experience in the UK.

For example, a Home Office study, which was undertaken in thirteen selected police areas during the summer of 1981, reported that people of Asian origin were fifty times more likely than white people to be the victims of racially motivated offences. In the case of the Afro-Caribbeans, the number of victims of racial incidents per thousand of the population was thirty-seven times higher than that of whites (Home Office 1981). The more recent report of the Inter-Departmental Racial Attacks Group notes that these forms of racist violence are simply the tip of the iceberg and that a range of seemingly trivial incidents, such as jostling in the street, racial abuse by children, and the daubing of racist graffiti, 'create an insidious atmosphere of racial harassment and intimidation' (Home Office 1989: para. 11).

It is not surprising, given these daily experiences, that about half of the Afro-Caribbean and South Asian respondents in Colin Brown's 1984 study should opine that 'life had become worse for their group' (Brown 1984: 247). This somewhat bleak appraisal, as Brown himself indicates, must be contrasted with the relatively sanguine views that were expressed by these groups in an earlier survey (Smith 1977). At that time, less than 20 per cent of black respondents indicated that 'race' relations had deteriorated.

The findings of the *British Social Attitudes* surveys in 1984 and 1985 are similarly disconcerting (see Jowell *et al.* 1986 for a discussion). In 1984, 'British Society' was described by more than 90 per cent of the 1,800 adults who were interviewed as: 'racially prejudiced against black and Asian members' (Jowell *et al.* 1986: 149). Two-thirds believed that these groups were subject to discrimination in employment, 40 per cent felt that racial prejudice in the UK had increased during the five years prior to the survey, and a third classified themselves as 'racially prejudiced'. There was a similar pattern of response in 1985. The research indicated that racial attitudes may vary with gender and political affiliation but there were 'no strong differences' between people of different ages and of different occupations' (Jowell *et al.* 1986: 150).

While the *British Social Attitudes* survey probably conveys a more accurate impression of contemporary 'race' relations than Furnham and Gunter (1989), neither study is able to shed any light upon the following questions. Why is racism fused with relevance by different groups of people in quite dissimilar circumstances? Why does it still persist despite offending conventional moral values? What are the characteristics of racist thinking or logic? Why does individual racism surface in 'all-white' areas as well as in ethnically mixed areas? Let us see what Ellis Cashmore's research tells us about these issues.

Youth and racism

Cashmore is not solely concerned with the impact of racism on the consciousness of youth in Thatcher's UK. His three-year study explores the racial attitudes of people from secondary school-age through to retirement, who are drawn from a variety of social and ethnic backgrounds. We shall focus on what Cashmore refers to as the 'visions of youth': that is, the perspectives on 'race' of those aged 21 or under. The bulk of those approached during the study came from four residential areas in the West Midlands: a working-class and a middle-class area close to the centre of Birmingham (Newtown and Edgbaston) and two comparable locations outside of the city (Chelmsley Wood and Solihull).

While we have reservations about Cashmore's methodology, the study is, nevertheless, a timely and important contribution to the literature on racism and socialization. Among other things, Cashmore is concerned to explain the *differentiated* response of white working-class youth to racism. To illustrate his argument, he compares and contrasts the attitudes, beliefs and biographies of two unemployed men: John is 20 and lives in multi-ethnic Newtown; 19-year old Kevin is living in predominantly white Chelmsley Wood. Both men come from similar blue-collar backgrounds, have similar educational experiences and have parents with 'compatible views on ethnic issues'. However, John and Kevin part company when racism is considered. For example, John finds no difficulty in empathizing with his black peers and is able to appreciate the fallaciousness of 'the classic 3 million unemployed = 3 million blacks and Asians equation'.

Unlike John, Kevin constantly employs racist epithets when referring to black people and, invariably, draws upon 'a limited repertoire of stereotypes' when describing either South Asians or Afro-Caribbeans. He blames ethnic minorities for a range of social problems, from deteriorating job prospects and declining living standards through to drug abuse. To account for their differing perspectives, Cashmore draws on the contact hypothesis which we discussed in Chapter 2. He argues that, although 'the idea of ethnic proximity as a recipe for ethnic harmony' should not be exaggerated, direct knowledge (or first-hand experience) of ethnic minorities can help to modify parental precepts and the racist images and myths that abound in the media and popular culture. According to Cashmore:

> John is unaffected by the worries of an Asian takeover of Newtown's shops, which seem to preoccupy his parents' generation. He has no fear of the stereotype black mugger who allegedly prowls the estate. *First hand experience* tells him a different story: 'It's a struggle for all of us as far as I'm concerned.' His *contact* with members of ethnic minorities obviates the need to resort to the stereotyped images so central to racism.
>
> (Cashmore 1987: 83; emphases added)

He goes on to remark that:

> John has grown up on an estate with a full ethnic mix, while

Kevin's interpersonal contacts have been restricted to a short – and as it turned out fiery – period in Birmingham with a black family as neighbours ('The old man ended up having a fight with the bloke') and a stretch in detention.

(Cashmore 1987: 86)

Cashmore's remarks about white middle-class youth in Edgbaston and Solihull concur with the claims of Billig and his colleagues (1988) concerning the tendency for the respectable (and reasonable) to avoid the more explicit forms of racist discourse. Cashmore's middle-class subjects, as well as contending that the Commission for Racial Equality (CRE) and others have provided a distorted picture of the influence of racism in the UK ('I don't think there's any deep discrimination'), generally appeared to espouse assimilationist positions, or interpreted 'race' relations in individualistic, rather than structural terms (Cashmore 1987: 95–105). Thus, he argues:

young people . . . living amidst the prosperity of middle class areas which afford a degree of protection from the more corrosive elements of inner-city life, have a benign and simplistic conception of race relations. The idea that the problem is much less than the media say it is; the willingness to apportion blame on the ethnics themselves opposed to the system in which they operate; the unflinching dogmaticism in defending the 'British way of life' as the norm to be adapted to, rather than a cultural process liable to change – all these are platitudes. In the absence of any meaningful sustained social intercourse, at school or after, middle class youth are bound to rely on worn out notions that are never tested out on reality.

(Cashmore 1987: 103–4)

The extent to which children and young people in ethnically mixed areas actually experience 'meaningful sustained social intercourse' with members of other ethnic groups remains open to question. As shown by the work on inter-ethnic friendship patterns in UK schools, a strong preference for own-group friends is generally established at an early age; where inter-ethnic friendships do occur, they rarely extend beyond the

classroom and playground to the home (Davey 1987). Notwithstanding this, we fully endorse Cashmore's strictures about the
particular importance of curricular initiatives in addressing the
issues of racism in the 'all-white' school. Unfortunately, as we
indicated in Chapter 1, not only have schools in these areas
remained resistant to anti-racist and multicultural education but
also many schools continue to embrace a 'colour-blind' approach
to the curriculum.

Cashmore's uncovering of racist interpretations of reality in
'all-white' areas is supported by other research. For instance,
Frank Coffield, Carol Borrill and Sarah Marshall (1986) provide
evidence of the prevalence of racism among young, working-
class people in north-east England: a region where ethnic
minorities form less than one per cent of the overall population.
Despite the limited first-hand experience of ethnic minorities of
many of the young men and women in the study, they held
'explicitly racist views, while others, who claimed not to be
racist, frequently made racist statements' (Coffield *et al.* 1986:
195–6). Although the youth in question often made derogatory
remarks about black people in general ('smarmy Pakis', 'lecher-
ous Iranians'), such stereotypes were invariably abandoned
when referring to individual group members, with whom they
had established a rapport: 'a Paki at our shop . . . he's dead
canny' (Coffield *et al.* 1986: 197). Whereas Coffield and his
colleagues dealt with the issue of racism tangentially, as a part of
a wider study of the lifestyles, attitudes and values of young
people 'growing up at the margins', other work which was
conducted in 'non-contact' areas has focused more directly on
this issue. For example, Winifred Mould's (1987) study of the
racial attitudes of 9-year olds, 13-year olds and sixth-formers in
Tyne and Wear was undertaken in an attempt to convince
senior teaching staff in the locality of the need for the LEA's
newly introduced policy on multicultural education. As an
advisory teacher, Mould wanted to obviate resistance to the
policy and to disabuse staff who expressed the view that 'there's
no problem here'. She invited about two hundred primary and
secondary school pupils to produce some 'cold' writing on the
topic of black people. Teachers were asked not to discuss this
work with the pupils; it was undertaken anonymously. Not

surprisingly, when encouraged to employ a racial frame of reference and to articulate racist attitudes and beliefs, the pupils obliged. A content analysis of the scripts revealed that about three-quarters of the pupils 'held negative attitudes about black people and, of those, one-third held strongly hostile attitudes' (Mould 1987: 51). Despite the obvious ethical and methodological shortcomings of Mould's work, it indicates that racism may be rife among young people attending 'all-white' (or predominantly white) schools. As shown by the evidence that was marshalled by the CRE in its report, *Learning in Terror*, racial harassment is not uncommon in 'non-contact' areas, such as the north east (CRE: 1988). The case studies which were outlined in the report serve to reinforce our claims about the importance of anti-racist teaching in the 'all-white' school and also lend support to the view that such teaching should begin at primary level.

Children and racism: catching them young?

Shahnaz Akhtar's study of the racial attitudes of children attending first and middle schools in Norwich also points to the presence of racist understandings in young children (Akhtar and Stronach 1986). Focusing on the experiences of pupils of South Asian descent, Akhtar found that racial name-calling and bullying started much earlier than teachers tend to assume: that is, between 4- and 5-years old. As the children grew older, these incidents became more frequent. Despite this, her research revealed that there was a general reluctance among teachers to acknowledge the extent, or sometimes even the existence, of racism in their schools:

'We don't have any problems in this school. Children accept them as friends.'

'We have no name-calling here. There might be in the playground.'

(Akhtar and Stronach 1986)

Akhtar is not alone in arguing this (Carrington and Short 1987; Carrington and Troyna 1988). Indeed, there may be a tendency for primary teachers to regard younger children as 'colour-blind' and free from the malign influence of racism, even though such perceptions have no foundation in reality.

Since the publication in the United States of the research by Bruno Lasker (1929) and Eugene Horowitz (1936), many studies have shown that very young children can be influenced by racism. Although teachers may claim that young children are largely unconscious of 'race', 'the ability to recognise and label racial differences and also to identify oneself in racial terms seems to be established between three and five years old', according to David Milner (1983: 108). He goes on to note that 'rudimentary feelings' about racial differences, including showing preference towards one's own group and hostility towards others, 'can also appear as early as three, though it is more usual at four to five years'. Between seven and nine years, as children begin to absorb 'more complex information about racial groups, stereotypes about their characteristics, and notions of social status', these rudimentary feelings develop into more fully fledged racial attitudes (Milner 1983: 110).

Because overt racism is generally regarded as lying beyond the parameters of respectability, children and young people are often ambivalent in their attitudes to 'race'. To illustrate this point, Billig and his colleagues recount an interview with Wendy (a 15-year old National Front supporter) and her friend (Billig *et al.* 1988). They show that both interviewees firmly 'believed that non-whites should be expelled from Britain' and made 'free use of stereotypes, as they described West Indians and Asians in simple terms'. Although Wendy displayed 'the signs which psychologists normally associate with prejudice', after the interview she was to be seen 'walking arm in arm with a young Asian girl, chatting and laughing in easy friendship' (Billig *et al.* 1988: 100–6). Jeffcoate's (1977) research in a Bradford nursery school also warrants attention, since it not only provides evidence of the early onset of incipient racism but also suggests that 4-year olds may already be aware that such behaviour lies beyond the bounds of respectability. He found that young children often made disparaging comments about black people but that such remarks were generally confined to the peer group; the presence of a teacher (or another adult authority figure) clearly had an inhibiting effect.

It follows from Geoffrey Short's work with primary school pupils that any initiative in anti-racist education must be framed in a way that is sensitive to young children's understanding and knowledge of 'race' (see Carrington and Short 1989: 59–80). Short interviewed 161 children, from the ages of 6–11, in two 'all-white' schools. As well as attempting to probe the children's knowledge of the impact of individual racism on the lives of black people in the UK, Short sought to explore their understanding of racial stereotyping, inequality and discrimination. He found that there was a marked disjunction between the responses of the 6- and 7-year olds and the remainder of the children in the sample. Whereas 8–11 year olds seemed to possess 'similar and relatively sophisticated ideas' about 'race' and racism, many of the infants had particularly 'immature views on the origin and biological significance of skin pigmentation'. For example, when 7-year old David was asked why some people are black and others white, he opined: 'Probably their mums were sunbathing and they got brown and the baby came out brown. If mums don't sunbathe, the baby comes out white.' Similarly, 6-year old Matthew believed that someone born black could become white 'if they have a bath' (Carrington and Short 1989: 65–6). Although 'a sizeable proportion' of this age group 'had little awareness of the everyday realities confronting black people', virtually all of the 8- and 9-year olds saw individual racism (in some form) as the 'most serious blight on a black child's life'. Among the 10- and 11-year olds, there was also an awareness of institutional racism as it is encountered by black adults, in employment and housing (Carrington and Short 1989: 68).

'Commonsense' racism and popular culture

Throughout this chapter we have stressed the entrenched nature of individual racism and its resilience to change (in all sectors of society). We have suggested that, whereas explicit forms of racism are now less likely to be socially sanctioned, more subtle and covert manifestations of the ideology remain commonplace. These more subtle forms are sustained through the process of disavowal: 'I'm not prejudiced, but . . . '. While first-hand experience of South Asian or Afro-Caribbean people may serve to modify some racial stereotypes, as we have indicated in our critique of the 'contact hypothesis', such experience cannot be seen as a panacea for racism. Experiential learning, whether in school or out, is unlikely to have any impact on the attitudes of the 'hard-core' racist. As Philip Cohen has remarked:

> For those who have a strong ontological stake in racism – who cannot stand the touch, sight, sound or smell of Black people – familiarity only 'breeds' more contempt; for the majority, material experiences of other cultures, however positive, do not seem to deconstruct negative stereotype.
>
> (Cohen 1988: 89)

We want to consider Cohen's work in some depth for the following reasons. First, he builds on existing research to describe and analyse the characteristics of individual racism and its transmission in popular culture. Second, he is concerned not merely with rarefied academic aims but rather with the aim of facilitating the development of effective anti-racist strategies both in education and in youth and community work. In common with other critics (e.g. Carter and Williams 1987; Hatcher 1987), Cohen argues that these strategies often lack a sufficiently solid conceptual foundation: racism tends to be conflated with prejudice and to be depicted as an illogical belief system, a form of intolerance and a product of ignorance. (As we have already pointed out, the New Right tends to view racism in this way, along with many liberal researchers, such as Furnham and Gunter 1989). This conception of racism, which informs the Swann report (DES 1985a) and the work of James Lynch (1987) on prejudice reduction, lends support to the view that racist beliefs can be dislodged simply through dialogue and an appeal to reason. According to this naïve view, teachers can counter racist arguments, in which black people are depicted as a scapegoat for material problems, by drawing pupils' attention to the 'true' causes of unemployment and the reasons for immigration. According to Cohen, however,

the problem with this kind of rationalist pedagogy is not just that it rests on an inadequate theory of racism; it fails to grasp the fact that popular racism does not rely on 'theories' in the sense of worked out beliefs about society. . . . The racist imagination constructs its own objects of perception and its own internal procedures of consensual validation in a way which is quite impervious to theoretic logic.

(Cohen 1988: 88)

How do we respond to Cohen's arguments about pedagogy? It seems to us that they place teachers in a somewhat invidious position. After all, by failing to engage directly with racist viewpoints in the classroom, teachers would find themselves vulnerable to the same criticisms as those levelled at Robert Jeffcoate (1979) and other proponents of what is known as the 'neutral chair' approach. Jeffcoate not only advocated that children should be permitted to articulate racist viewpoints during class discussion but also suggested that teachers should avoid adopting a censorious attitude in such cases. By regarding such viewpoints as having the same status and validity as others, Jeffcoate has rightly been criticized for condoning racism by default. While Cohen is correct to stress that counter-arguments to racism are unlikely to have an impact on pupils with pronounced racist views, other pupils with more equivocal and contradictory positions (such as those described by Billig *et al.* [1988] as the 'reasonably prejudiced'), may be less 'impervious' to an anti-racist perspective.

'My kind of town'

Cohen's starting-point is that territorial claims often provide a focal point of racism in working-class communities, especially among males. For the economically and politically marginal, one's place of origin confers 'special quasi-magical forms of ownership and control' (Cohen 1988: 33). Taking the example of London's East End, Cohen argues that those 'born and bred' in this area have tended to look upon it as their 'own'. In general, they regard others as 'outsiders' and, as such, a potential threat to their identity and well-being. This illusion of 'owner-ship and control' was shattered by the arrival of black immigrants during the 1950s and 1960s. Their entry into the local labour and housing markets served to stimulate the development of racial scapegoating (and other forms of racism) by exposing the relative powerlessness of the white East Enders. The presence of black people in this part of London showed that the white working class did not 'own' (or 'control') jobs or neighbourhoods. By highlighting the illusory nature of this aspect of working-class consciousness, 'the immigrant unconsciously came to represent' the *real* structures of power in society, which are 'disavowed' (Cohen 1988: 34).

Rumour and humour: the transmission of racist thinking

Another part of Cohen's argument about individual racism centres on the role of humour. Because verbal abuse provides popular racist discourse with its 'cutting edge', Cohen shows how racist epithets often rely on myths and stereotypes about black people. To illustrate his argument, he examines the case of the 'jungle bunny', a 'monster' which, he claims, 'sprang to linguistic life, and spread (or bred) until it became the most popular term of abuse directed by white working class youth against Black people'. Cohen goes on to argue that this particular epithet

> links a popular racist myth (Blacks come from the jungle) to popular sexual fantasies (Blacks breed like rabbits) to force a racist misrecognition (Blacks are animals). The insult also contains an embedded injunction (Blacks should go back to the jungle where they belong).
>
> (Cohen 1988: 80)

The word 'bunny' (in isolation) has several connotations in white working-class youth culture, as Cohen's discussion with a group of hard-core racists suggests. When the young men were asked about this epithet, they told Cohen that 'bunny' meant 'slag' or 'whore'; it also signified someone who is gullible ('easily conned') or who is 'timid, or fearful and scared of authority (as in the popular song "Run, rabbit, run")'. In addition, the term described someone who is 'all mouth' and who 'rabbits on'. The term 'bunny', therefore, 'encompasses all the attributes most despised in these lads' culture'. Cohen shows how the epithet is used in a racist insult ('jungle bunny') to trap the victim in a 'double bind':

> If a Black boy is called a jungle bunny by one of these young racists, he may choose to ignore the insult and walk away. But that 'only proves' to the lads' satisfaction that Blacks are 'running scared'; if, however, he loses his temper and threatens to hit them, then that only goes to show that 'Blacks can't take a joke', and are 'no better than savages'. If he 'bad names' them back, then walks off, 'Blacks are all mouth'. No matter which way he responds, he confirms that he *is* a 'jungle bunny' in their eyes.
>
> (Cohen 1988: 81)

Incidents such as this occur daily in many school playgrounds (Home Office 1989; CRE 1988). What is more, there would appear to be a link between the more overt forms of individual racism and prevailing notions of masculinity, especially in 'rough' working-class culture, where male hierarchies tend to be based on physical strength and prowess. David Widgery's (1986) observation about the death of Altab Ali providing his black attacker with 'his ticket of admission into white male society' bears testimony to this. Racism and anti-Semitism are rife on the terraces at many football grounds, which, of course, are largely male bastions (Williams *et al.* 1984). This is not surprising, because football continues to provide working-class males with not only a medium for the celebration of masculinity but also a context for the expression of local identities and loyalties. As Mike Brake has put it:

> Territory has an importance symbolically in youth cultures among the working class. Pride in the local territory becomes an expression of conservatism, with the protection of it flaring into racism and prejudice. Symbolically, it can also manifest itself in the defence by the violent of its 'turf', or in the aggressive support for local football teams.
>
> (Brake 1980: 37)

The structure of racist arguments

Cohen suggests that racist arguments tend to have the following characteristic forms. The scapegoating of black people for declining job prospects stems from the false assumption that two unrelated historical events – the arrival of black people in the UK (or the locality) and mounting unemployment – are in some way causally connected. The spurious conclusion that 'Blacks are taking our jobs' is then drawn. Other racist arguments are based on false syllogisms. (A syllogism is a deductive argument in which a conclusion is derived from two given, or assumed, propositions called premises.) Cohen provides two examples of racist ascription or stereotyping to illustrate this point. In the first of these false syllogisms, the term 'some' is expunged from the initial premise; in the second, ascription occurs through 'the identification of subjects by predicates':

> [Some] young Blacks are criminals.
> Errol is a young Black.
> Therefore Errol is a thief.

> Criminals are people who fail to conform to society.
> Rastas are people who fail to conform to society.
> Therefore Rastas are criminals.

(Cohen 1988: 90–1)

If teachers are to engage effectively with this 'logic', then consideration must be given to the medium as well as to its message when devising curricular interventions. Pupils will thus be better placed to explore questions relating to social justice, equality and human rights if they are in a democratic setting where they feel confident in their relations with each other and with the teacher. An authoritarian environment, where the views of the pupils are marginalized or suppressed and where classroom talk is dominated by the teacher, is unlikely to do anything to facilitate the development of critical thinking, reflexivity or empathy. We shall return to these issues in greater detail in Chapter 5.

In this chapter, we have drawn upon various studies to show that racism is not simply an expression of individual prejudice or intolerance, despite what Margaret Thatcher, Sir Keith

Joseph and Ray Honeyford have to say. We have also noted the resilience of racism and that racism pervades all age groups and social classes. It therefore follows that anti-racist education needs to be introduced in all primary and secondary schools, irrespective of ethnic composition or locality. While we recognize that racist attitudes and beliefs (along with others) are subject to a range of influences beyond the school, including the media, family and peer group, the role of education in socialization should not be understated. As Cashmore observes:

> Clearly, the influence of the school on a child's values, beliefs and perceptions varies according to class, area and age. The precise degree of influence relative to other factors like the family and peer groups is virtually impossible to establish. Education nevertheless has a central role to play in race relations. It cannot reach adults who are convinced of the rightness of their values and superiority of their beliefs. But it can affect the judgement and perception of future generations.
>
> (Cashmore 1987: 221)

Discussion points

1 The 'rotten apple theory of racism' supports the view of the UK as being an essentially tolerant society. In the light of your reading, can this perception be sustained?
2 Racism, sexism and other controversial issues are often seen as 'taboo' in the primary school. Do you think that teachers are justified in avoiding discussion of these matters with younger children?

4 The Education Reform Act 1988: to free or not to free?

Political or politicized education?

'For good or ill', writes Godfrey Brandt in *The Realization of Anti-Racist Teaching*, 'probably the most important document to emerge within the discourse of race and education is the Swann report' (Brandt 1987: 61–2). Few would disagree with this view. As we saw in Chapter 2, the Swann report, *Education for All*, was the outcome of an inquiry into the education of children from ethnic minority groups. The committee was convened in 1979 by Shirley Williams, then Labour's Secretary of State for Education, and in its first two years was chaired by Anthony Rampton. Although we offer a different interpretation of its origins, ostensibly its brief was to put flesh on the bones of the DES commitment to multicultural education, which had been expressed publicly for the first time in the 1977 Green Paper, *Education in Schools: A Consultative Document*. Shirley Williams remembers the initiative thus:

> It was straightforward enough to call for a curriculum and textbook that reflected a modern world of independent states rather than an Imperial aftermath. I did so myself in the 1977 Green Paper that called for a core curriculum reflecting the cultural and ethnic diversity of our country and its interdependence with the wider world. Bringing it about, where resources were limited and becoming more so, where few new teachers were being recruited because of falling rolls in the schools, was a much more difficult proposition.
>
> (Williams 1989: viii)

In her view, *Education for All* has succeeded in confirming the legitimacy of multicultural education as a conception of reform which has implications for all schools, irrespective of the ethnic mix of the pupil population or the location. For Williams, the Swann report is 'the boldest, most comprehensive statement on the subject' of multicultural education (Williams 1989: vii). Whilst there is broad agreement about its significance and status, not everyone, however, has greeted its publication in euphoric terms. Brandt traces reactions to the report along a continuum. At one extreme are cries of 'racist rubbish'; at the other, 'the best thing since sliced bread'. Between them is the view: 'can do better – should try harder' (Brandt 1987: 63). There is not enough space here to consider these responses in detail; however, the collections edited by Chivers (1987) and Verma (1989) give some flavour of these differential viewpoints.

On the face of it, it might be difficult to appreciate why organizations, such as NAME (1985), or educational critics, such as Carter and Williams (1987), Mullard (1986) and Troyna (1986; 1989), should be so hostile towards the report. After all, it has helped to diffuse the significance of multicultural education to areas which, prior to its publication, had tended to distance themselves from this educational orthodoxy and to remain stubbornly committed to a 'no problem here' posture on 'race' and schooling. In the process, it has played an important role in enhancing the status of cultural pluralism as an informing principle of contemporary educational policy and practice. Time and again, journals such as *Multicultural Teaching* publish articles by exponents of multicultural education in all-white/ non-contact areas who refer to the Swann report as the peg on which they have hung their argument. What is more, the post-Swann period has witnessed some movement at central government level for funding initiatives along multicultural lines. Between 1986–9, for instance, 'Teaching and the Curriculum in a Multi-Ethnic Society' was a national priority area for the in-service training grants scheme. Central government has also awarded education support grants for pilot projects to improve the response of the education service to ethnic and cultural diversity. Alongside these initiatives have been moves to

encourage teacher education courses to develop students' understanding of multicultural education and to increase opportunities for black students of Afro-Caribbean and South Asian
origin to qualify for and enter teaching. It therefore seems that
central and local governments have, on the whole, responded
positively to Swann's song of 'Education for All', so why has the
report been disparaged?

In our opinion, the Swann report has achieved nothing more
than to encourage the promotion and legitimation of certain
versions of multicultural education; put differently, it has
precipitated few, if any, discernible changes to the ideological
terrain on which central and local governments premise their
policies on 'race' and education. To all intents and purposes, the
various post-Swann initiatives which we have described can be
distilled into two distinctive but mutually supportive ideological
frames. First, an increasing number of LEAs and education
institutions have been persuaded to accept cultural pluralism as
a legitimate concern in the formulation of policies. From this
viewpoint, Swann has been 'a landmark in pluralism' (Verma
1989). Second, more and more education administrators and
practitioners have recognized the need to develop guidelines for
dealing with the perpetrators and victims of racial harassment.
Although these developments might be seen as worthwhile, it
does seem fair to ask if they represent anything more or less
than is expected in a liberal democratic society. After all, as we
have already seen in this book, a pre-eminent concern in
contemporary, mainstream debates on 'race relations' has been
to maintain a guise of reasonableness. Therefore, to reject
Swann's song of cultural pluralism (and the celebration of ethnic
minority lifestyles which it prescribes) would be to degenerate
into and to legitimate a virulent and *unreasonable* brand of
assimilationism. Similarly, to sanction racial harassment, by
either omission or commission, would be incompatible with a
cornerstone of liberal democracy, namely, the protection and
security of individual liberties and welfare. Thus what has been
seized from *Education for All* are those very recommendations
which lend themselves to the state's self-image of a 'tolerant'
society where manifestations of racist behaviour are deemed to
be unacceptable and to be restricted to a few 'bone-headed'

extremists. Put another way, The Three S's (Saris, Samosas and Steel bands), 'the rotten apple theory of racism' and the contact hypothesis have all received the benediction of the Swann report. In its aftermath, they, above all else, represent the templates within which initiatives are compelled to fit if they are to receive economic and political backing from central government (Ball and Troyna 1989).

The other side of this coin, however, is a continued avoidance of the question of how the educational system might respond effectively to racist impulses in society at large. The Swann committee circumvented this problem by identifying racism primarily in terms of individual prejudice and by recommending Racism Awareness Training (RAT) as a way of correcting cultural misunderstandings. The notion of institutionalized racism, in contrast, was considered 'confused and confusing' by the committee, which at the same time was convinced that state institutions are 'in no way racist in intent' (DES 1985a: 28). Should we be surprised by this sanguine view of state institutions? Perhaps not. As Ahmed Gurnah argues, we should see committees such as this as state gatekeepers and caretakers. Their role is to defend the United Kingdom and 'the idea of it: it is their duty to do so'. As he goes on to say: 'They are defending the system, its root as well as its future. They defend a way of life' (Gurnah 1987: 24). This is a seductive argument and helps to explain why Lord Swann's predecessor, Anthony Rampton, 'resigned' after the publication of the committee's interim report (DES 1981). Despite its subscribing to an array of pathological interpretations of black education 'underachievement' – poor family background, lack of parental support, inadequate socialization – the Rampton report gave space to institutionalized racism as a contributory factor in this process. This was hardly the interpretation that was expected or wanted from a custodian of the state!

Despite our critical judgement on the Swann report and our reservations about the initiatives that it has spawned, its support for political education gave some semblance of hope to anti-racist conceptions of reform. The broadly conceived programme of political education which Swann and his colleagues outlined in the report provided the potential to displace 'the rotten apple', individualized view of racism in contemporary British society. What is more, it recognized that the medium as well as the message must be incorporated into models of anti-racist education. The committee recommended that all schools should engage openly and directly with issues of racism and should consider the origins of racial inequality within a wider programme of political education. As part of 'good' education, Swann encouraged schools to provide pupils with

> the ability to accept a range of differing and possibly conflicting points of view and to argue rationally and independently about the principles which underlie these, free from pre-conceived prejudices or stereotypes, and to recognise and resist false arguments and propaganda. . . .
>
> If youngsters are to reflect critically on the political framework of life in this country, this should involve a consideration of how particular structures and procedures have evolved and their appropriateness to today's multi-racial population. . . . Effective political education should also lead youngsters to consider fundamental issues such as social justice and equality and this in turn should cause them to reflect on the origins and mechanism of racism and prejudice at an individual level.

(DES 1985a: 335–6)

Here, of course, the Swann committee perceived a close link between the health and stability of the democratic, multiracial society and the willingness of schools to prepare young people for their role as citizens. This fitted neatly with the views of Robert Dunn, who, as Under-Secretary of State for Education, had nailed his colours to the mast of political education in a speech to the Politics Association in 1984. As well as endorsing the argument that political education would encourage young people to appraise critically 'different viewpoints' and 'conflicting motives', Dunn insisted that pupils' perception of and experience in the school setting would influence the direction and shape of their political attitudes:

> The organisation of the school and the teaching methods employed within it will have an effect. The way in which

pupils' own views are received within a school, by other
pupils and by the staff, can contribute to those pupils'
development or can inhibit it.

(Dunn 1984: 295)

Along with the Swann committee, Dunn's conception of political education in schools went well beyond the mechanistic
approach to tackling negative racial attitudes that was favoured
by rationalist pedagogues such as Lynch (1987). Indeed, it
corresponds more closely with the analysis that was provided by
Phil Cohen, whose work we discussed in Chapter 3. Dunn gave
credence to an holistic programme of political education in all
schools by stressing the roles that pedagogy, organizational
norms and classroom encounters might play in shaping and
buttressing political attitudes.

The radical complexion of these proposals fell on stony
ground, however. The government, in its White Paper, *Better
Schools,* agreed with Swann and others that 'the principles of
freedom, justice and tolerance will be most effectively applied in
our national life if they are soundly established at school' (DES
1985b: 62). However, this passage sat uneasily in a document
which presaged the reconstruction of the curriculum along
traditional subject lines and in which the apparent politicization
of education was both lamented and criticized. It is ironic that
the Swann report was published in early 1985, around the same
time as *Better Schools* and *Education and Indoctrination,* the latter comprising a polemical attack on schools and
LEAs by Roger Scruton and his colleagues on the New Right.
Relying heavily on what is known as the 'totalizing fallacy',
whereby broad generalizations are drawn on the basis of one or
two 'illustrative' and 'representative' cases, Scruton and his co-
writers argued that education in the mid-1980s had become too
political or, to be more precise, politicized and that central
government needed to take urgent steps to curtail the
(perceived) incursion of the Left into the curriculum and
organization of schools. According to this view, political indoctrination had been achieved through the introduction of subjects
such as Peace Studies, 'whose main purpose is to project a
particular set of attitudes', and in the politicization (or

subversion) of existing subjects (Scruton *et al.* 1985: 7). For these polemicists, schools under the proliferating influence of left-wing radicals 'are exceeding the limited authority conferred on them by the 1944 Education Act'. Set alongside the inexorable growth of a 'para-educational establishment' (i.e. LEA advisers and administrators), Scruton and his associates identified what they saw as an insidious trend which needed to be curtailed, by means of stronger direction from the centre, to ensure 'the maintenance of standards in education' (Scruton *et al.* 1985: 49).

Better Schools also centralized the issue of standards. According to this document, greater consideration needed to be given to 'accountability', 'relevance', 'national needs' and 'competence'. This would guarantee that 'the education of the pupils serves their own and the country's needs and provides a fair return to those who pay for it' (DES 1985b: 4). Although less hysterical than *Education and Indoctrination,* the 1985 White Paper was equally committed to the aggrandizement of central control over the shape and orientation of the education system. As we shall see in the next section, the enhancement of central powers, and a correlative decline in the influence of 'professionals' in the classrooms and in county halls, is axiomatic to the Thatcher government's vision of what Ira Shor (1986) calls the 'conservative restoration' of educational principles. It is a vision which has been expedited through the 1988 Education Reform Act.

Loosening the bonds

After Kenneth Baker had presided over the Education Reform Act (ERA), a piece of legislation which comprised 238 clauses and 13 schedules and which attracted more parliamentary time than any other legislation in the post-war period, he declared that it marked 'the beginning of a new era' *(The Times,* 30 July 1988). Even the most vociferous opponents of the Act would agree. Consider, for instance, how Richard Johnson sums up its significance:

> I believe that the main configurations of formal schooling will be unrecognizable by the mid 1990s in many respects: the powers of local education authorities (LEAs), for exam-

ple; the balance of public and private provision; the role of
the central state. . . . The transition will be as fundamental as
that of 1780–1840 (the birth of 'mass schooling') or as that of
1865–80 (the creation of a civic education service). By the
end of the century the 'growth' of 1870–1970 may look like a
specific historical phase, with its typical educational forms
oddly relative to my children's children.

(Johnson 1989: 92).

In broad terms, the ERA leads to a fundamental reconstitution of
the institutional framework in which schools and colleges reside.
With Johnson, we see this initiative both as revolutionary and
irreversible. On the one hand, it provides for a massive shift
towards strong direction and control from the centre, through the
introduction of a National Curriculum with targets of attainment
and assessment at ages 7, 11, 14 and 16. In all, it delegates over
400 new powers to the Secretary of State for Education. On the
other hand, it allows for greater devolution of power to parents
and governors over the way in which schools (and colleges) are
organized, funded and governed. With the creation of City
Technology Colleges (CTCs), the introduction of open enrolment and, in cases where a majority of parents, governors and the
Secretary of State are in agreement, the opportunity for schools
to 'opt out' of local authority control, assume grant maintained
status (GMS) and obtain funding directly from Whitehall, the
ERA formalizes a system where market forces seem to prevail.
How do we make sense of an initiative which champions both
interventionist ('strong' government) and *laissez-faire* ('weak')
models of control? To begin with, we see the National
Curriculum and associated tests of attainment as a means to an
end rather than as an end in themselves. That is to say, we see
them functioning primarily as a regulatory mechanism to ensure,
as far as possible, that this more diverse, or stratified, system of
schooling does not degenerate into chaos and disorder. It is a pre-
emptory strategy, first and foremost; it is less a check on the
pupils than a check on the system.

However, whether it is through the celebration of 'parent
power' and the atomization of decision-making which this
denotes, or through the extension of centralized control, the

'loosening of bonds of local authority control of schools and their pupils' (Morris and Griggs 1988: 15) must provide the interpretive lens through which we can give coherence and logic to these ostensibly disparate proposals. The ERA is the culmination of a trend which is aimed at undercutting the power base of LEAs. This process, during the Thatcherite years, has involved two discrete but related phases: first, the raising as a legitimate question of the right of LEAs to influence the structure, orientation and content of education; second, the abolition of LEAs. On the first of these, Mrs Thatcher indicated to delegates at the 1987 annual Conservative party conference that the powers of LEAs were not carved in tablets of stone; 'There's no reason at all why local authorities should have a monopoly of free education. What principle suggests this is right?' (Thatcher 1987: 8). Even before this declaration of intent there had been subtle indications that LEAs would be emasculated in the realignment of central–local relations in education. For example, the 1981 edition of the DES's *Brief Guide* to the education service opens with a chapter entitled 'A National Service Locally Administered' and starts by asserting that: 'The tradition of decentralised education in Britain is strong'. In the 1984 edition of this pamphlet, both the chapter heading and opening sentence have been deleted. Instead, we are told that: 'The Department of Education and Science is responsible for all aspects of education in England' (cited in Simon 1988). Mrs Thatcher made clear, in an interview reported in the *Daily Mail* in the pre-1987 election period, that her third administration would accelerate this process and would mount a more overt, less inhibited attack on LEAs. As she informed the paper's editor, David English,

> It will be possible to get some of these schools out of the local authorities and have direct grants from the Department of Education. . . . Fortunately we still have the powers. I don't like what is going on. And that is exactly why we would be taking away the powers from the local authorities in these cases.
>
> (*Daily Mail*, 13 May 1987)

As the most succinct, public expression of the Conservative

party's education policy, the ERA must be viewed as an integral part of a broader government strategy which is geared towards central omniscience. It therefore extends and supports the other main elements in the party's third-term legislative programme. From the Local Government Finance Act, which replaces the rates with a community charge (or poll tax) and uniform business rate, through to the Housing Act which allows council tenants to 'opt out' of local authority management and control; from the Local Government Act, which obliges local councils to put out their catering, cleaning and other services to competitive tendering and, in Section 27, bans them from publishing publicity material which might be deemed as 'political', through to the ERA and its redesignation of powers for LEAs, we are witnessing a scenario in which those who work in (or are elected to) county halls have become agents rather than partners of central government. As Eric Pickles, leader of the Conservative council in Bradford, explained, his ideas for the radical reconstruction of local government along Thatcherite lines could not have been realized *before* the third term, the reason being that:

> It all comes together because of the Education Act, the Housing Bill, compulsory competitive tendering and the community charge.
> We have had all these various things from up high, from the Government, to set a framework. Now what we have to do is to start reforming local government from within.
>
> (*Guardian*, 22 October 1988).

What is the likely impact of the ERA, and the systemic changes that it prescribes, on the struggle for racial equality in education? Does the legislation formally mark the end to 'the pursuit of egalitarianism', as Kenneth Baker assured his colleagues in 1987? We shall explore this later in this chapter and in Chapter 5. Before then, let us spend some time examining in more detail the origins and development of the ERA.

The sleight of hand

As the 1990s begin and the ERA emerges from the statute book to become part of the living reality of classrooms and staffrooms throughout the UK, various commentators have made attempts to periodize the development of Conservative education policy since the election of Mrs Thatcher in May 1979. Richard Johnson, for instance, has identified five distinct periods in which the fortunes of the Tory campaign for radical education reforms waxed and waned before reaching a high point in the passing of the ERA (Johnson 1989: 111–12). Geoff Whitty and Ian Menter (1989), on the other hand, pinpoint two main phases. The first extends from 1979 to April 1987, incorporating the first two administrations. In this phase, according to Whitty and Menter, 'opinion-moulding' was the name of the game. The pre-eminent concern was to excite public indignation about, and opposition to, LEA administrators, schools and their teachers. This was done with the complicity of the media, especially the tabloid press, and by excessive reliance on what we referred to earlier as the totalizing fallacy. It became *de rigueur* to denunciate LEAs and many of their schools and to characterize their (perceived) priorities and actions as 'loony left'. This is the period in which stories about 'Baa-Baa Green Sheep' and 'Race Spies' and a range of homophobic and sexist headlines saturated the media. Whitty and Menter suggest that the second phase was sparked off by the election of Mrs Thatcher to a third term of office in May 1987. Although they see the 1980 Education Act and 1986 Education (No. 2) Act as important in increasing the responsibility of 'the users' (parents and governors) at the expense of 'the producers' (administrators and teachers) of education, they suggest that it is only in the third term that legislation became the main tool of education policy.

Although periodization of the Thatcherite years helps us to grasp the development of Conservative party policy on education during the 1980s, both Johnson and Whitty and Menter recognize that the seeds of the ERA (and the radical changes to education which it heralds) were sown before the election of Thatcher in 1979. In order to understand the success of the Tories' education policy we must look more closely at the preceding period: when James Callaghan's Labour government held the reins of power.

Michael Apple has made the important point that 'one of the

tendencies of corporate economies when they are in crisis is to *export* the blame from the economy to the state' (Apple 1986: 17). A clear example of this ideological sleight of hand in policy in recent years has been the way in which the rise in (youth) unemployment has been 'explained'. The economy is not posed as the problem. Rather, it is schools and their failure to provide students with the appropriate skills or disposition which are held responsible (Walker and Barton 1986).

Against this background it is possible to understand the significance of James Callaghan's speech at Ruskin College, Oxford in 1976 and the ensuing 'Great Debate' on the post-war development of education policy in the UK. Callagham, with his emphasis on the instrumental role of education and his calls for a core curriculum, regular evaluation and assessment, set the scene for the onslaught of a series of regressive educational initiatives which has culminated in the ERA of 1988. Why did this happen?

The mid-1970s saw a major crisis surrounding the UK's balance of payments. The decision of the OPEC countries to quadruple oil prices caused a panic in which education was singled out as the culprit in, and potential saviour of, the UK's ailing economy. In precisely the way that Michael Apple suggests, the economic crisis of the mid-1970s was interpreted largely in terms of the failure of the state's educational system to deliver the goods. Callaghan's speech at Ruskin College in 1976 constituted public affirmation of a government losing faith with its education system. In his view, schools were failing to meet 'the goals of education'. These he saw as equipping 'children to the best of their ability for a lively, constructive place in society and also to fit them to do a job of work' (Callaghan 1976: 333). Callaghan also assigned credibility and legitimacy to views which until then had been consigned to the margins. Although he insisted that his plea for a return to 'formal instruction', for the introduction of a core curriculum and monitoring of resources, and for a re-evaluation of the traditional partnership in education was not 'a clarion call to the Black Paperites' (Callaghan 1976: 333), this is precisely what it was. As Brian Cox, co-editor of the ultra-conservative Black Papers, pointed out soon after the speech:

When we first started we were putting forward completely unacceptable ideas. But eventually we brought about the things Callaghan and the Education Secretary Shirley Williams are doing at the moment. The *Black Papers* have been the most important influence, though there have been others.

(Cited in Mack 1977: 589)

In the newly aligned policy agenda, 'how' was to assume more importance than 'why' and themes which linked the educational process inextricably to the economy were to become increasingly influential in determining how, when and where resources were to be allocated. Simply put, the interpretation of education as training was to assume increasing plausibility and influence on policy formulation.

The Great Debate did not appear out of thin air, however. We need to ask why it was that the Black Paper movement took centre stage seven years after the publication of its first document. It seems to us that its 'success' was secured through the dramatic events of 1975–6. Amongst these, the publication of Neville Bennett's report, *Teaching Styles and Pupil Progress* (1976) was especially important. Ostensibly, the book provided the first empirical insight into the efficacy or otherwise of child-centred education in primary schools. By any standards the launching of the book had to be viewed as a success. Even for a topic which was guaranteed to arouse professional, public and media interest, the blanket coverage was impressive. However, this was only part of the story. What was actually said in the media was of greater significance. Without exception, the media juxtaposed (good) formal teaching with (bad) informal, or 'progressive', approaches, despite Bennett's objections to this simplistic dichotomy. Headlines such as 'The Trendy Flop' and 'Pupils in Danger' *(Daily Express)* were manna from heaven for the Black Paperites. As Brian Cox acknowledged, the report 'vindicated everything we have been saying'. However, the attack on these post-Plowden, child-centred initiatives came from other sources. As Frank Musgrove (1987) has noted, Sharp and Green's study of 'Mapledene Lane' infant school was also heavily critical of 'progressive education'. From their perspective, 'the radicalism of the "progressive educator" ' could be viewed as 'a modern form of conservatism' (Sharp and Green 1975: viii). Both studies clearly influenced the educational landscape but the lie of the land was irrevocably altered by the furore in 1975 at the Islington junior school, William Tyndale.

A dispute arose there when the head and members of his staff encouraged child-centred learning in the school. They justified their decision in terms of teacher autonomy; that is, their right under the 1944 Education Act to determine what is taught and how it is taught in the school. However, the implementation of their ideas caused divisions within and beyond the school and Tyndale became the subject of a long and expensive official inquiry. The outcome was that the head and five teachers were sacked and another teacher resigned. At the heart of the matter was the question: who controls schools? As Roger Dale suggests, the Tyndale affair revealed how 'the pursuit of national economic goals could not be merely ignored but actually frustrated in a system where clear central leadership was absent' (Dale 1981: 310). The Tyndale affair sparked off a 'moral panic' about the 'corrosive' influence of progressive, egalitarian reforms on the education and moral standards in 'our' schools. Television and press reporters fell over themselves in the rush to find more examples of anarchy and indiscipline in primary and secondary schools, especially those which espoused progressive ideals. The next destination on the whistle-stop tour of blackboard jungles was Faraday comprehensive school in West London, the subject of a *Panorama* special in March 1977. The totalizing fallacy was now in full swing!

According to John Gretton and Mark Jackson of *The Times Educational Supplement,* this moral panic in general and the Tyndale affair in particular forewarned Secretaries of State for Education of the collapse of the system in the continued absence of centralized control.

> The main ingredients of William Tyndale could be found all over the country: a staff with strong radical convictions, a weak headteacher, a dithering inspectorate, worried parents and a local education authority that did not know what was

wanted of its primary schools. The mixture was common enough, but previously it had not been thought of as dangerously explosive. The *Zeitgeist,* however, had changed.

(Gretton and Jackson 1976: 121)

We agree. In the ambience that was generated by the mid-1970s economic crisis and that was exacerbated by the 'moral panic' surrounding the organization and activities of the nation's schools, the education system was to be assigned a more restrictive role, more in tune with the needs of the economy. This demanded that, even within the structurally decentralized system that was brought about through the 1944 Act, the centre should assume a more rigorous and custodial role. At the same time, the 'secret garden' of the school curriculum had to be prized open to ensure that schools adhered more rigidly to their new roles and set of expectations. Of course, all of this contrasted sharply with the optimism of the previous decade when egalitarian reforms flourished and were, in the main, supported throughout the educational community.

We are arguing, therefore, that the antecedents of the ERA reside in the economic crisis of the mid-1970s and the political response that it evoked. Amongst other things, the Tyndale affair and the subsequent 'moral panic' not only highlighted what were now to be seen as major deficiencies in the institutional framework that was established by the 1944 Education Act but also offered a rationale and blueprint for a major restructuring of the system. This would be an evolutionary change, culminating in the ERA and its provision for massive enhancement of power for the Secretary of State for Education. As we have indicated, the corollary has been a decline in the influence of teachers and, in particular, of LEAs over schools, colleges and the curriculum. Section 23 of the 1944 Act had given LEAs responsibility for control of the 'secular curriculum' in their local schools; Tyndale had demonstrated the difficulty which LEAs might experience in putting this into practice within a decentralized model. It had also demonstrated that the relative autonomy that was enjoyed both in classrooms and in county halls offered enormous potential for local regimes to ignore, depart from, or subvert this arrangement. If this scenario encouraged a move towards central direction, the furore at Tyndale also indicated that parents were likely to support the restoration of formal, even traditional models of organization, teaching and administration. In other words, it underlined the interplay between the conservative discourse on education, which was being articulated with increasing fervour at the centre, and the demands of many parents over what they expected from their children's schools (see Cullingford 1984, for instance).

'Apostles and bigots'

'It is the professional Left that now confronts us', Michael Heseltine informed his colleagues at the 1982 annual Conservative party conference *(Daily Mail,* 8 October). He was right. In a system of government which continued to allow a considerable degree of local discretion in the specification of objectives, the formulation of policies and the allocation of resources, the potential for resistance to centralized priorities constituted an important threat. More specifically, 'the triangle of tension' around the issue of who controls the schools needed to be addressed urgently. In dealing with the teachers, the strategy which has been deployed by Mrs Thatcher's various Secretaries of State for Education (Mark Carlisle, Sir Keith Joseph and Kenneth Baker) has been direct and uncomplicated; namely, a full-frontal attack on their powers of representation and negotiation. The former were abolished effectively in 1984 through the closure of the Schools Council and its replacement by two bodies, the Secondary Examinations Council (SEC) and the School Curriculum Development Council (SCDC), neither of which includes teacher representation. With the 1987 Teachers' Pay and Conditions Act came the abolition of the pay negotiation rights of the teaching profession and the imposition of new conditions of service and a new salaries structure.

LEAs, which were characterized by Kenneth Baker as 'apostles of mediocrity and bigots of indoctrination' in his speech to the 1987 annual Conservative party conference, have been the targets of a (slightly) more subtle but no less effective strategy of attrition. This has centred on two main tactics: circumvention and destabilization. Regarding the former, we can point to the way in which LEAs have been progressively marginalized in policy-making during the Thatcherite years. As Brian Simon put it in 1984, 'instead of working through and with other social organisations [the Conservative government] is now very clearly seeking a more direct and unitary system of control' (Simon 1984: 21). In the pre-ERA years, this tendency to circumvent negotiations with LEAs (and teacher unions) was exemplified in the manner by which the Technical and Vocational Education Initiative (TVEI) was introduced. As the brainchild of David Young, erstwhile chair of the Manpower Services Commission, TVEI was intended as a 'short, sharp, shock' to the education system. The ERA extends and strengthens this tendency to circumvent LEAs in establishing policy and practice. The setting up of CTCs, the opportunity for schools to 'opt out' of LEA management structures and the move towards open enrolment, which allows parents (rather than LEAs) to determine which schools their children will attend, all point in the same direction. The destabilization of local authorities has been secured through two main routes. The playing of 'loony left' tunes in the media and on various public platforms has, as we have argued, stirred up a 'moral panic' about how far LEAs encourage 'anti-family, anti-police and anti-competitive values in schools', as Kenneth Baker put it to conference in 1987. The construction of this 'moral panic' paved the way for the apparently legitimate questioning of the way in which local councils (especially those which were socialist) organized, funded and staffed their educational (and other social) services. In the case of the ILEA, of course, reasoning along these lines provided the context for its ultimate disintegration from April 1990.

A complementary move in the destabilizing of LEAs has seen successive Thatcher administrations alter the rules and procedures for funding local authorities. The norm is now prescriptive rather than permissive funding. Placed in the context of rate-capping (initiated by the 1984 Rates Act) and the community charge, both of which limit the amount that local councils can raise through taxes, the trend towards prescriptive funding demonstrates that local authorities are increasingly compelled to operate within the boundaries established by the centre. As education is the largest spender in local authorities, accounting for between 50–60 per cent of the annual budget, it is especially vulnerable to the constraints and demands for accountability which are implied by the move towards prescriptive funding. Simply put, educational initiatives are defined and confined by centrally defined priorities and concerns (see Troyna 1990).

The ERA: reform or deform?

In this chapter we have argued that the ERA will lead to a massive reduction in the role and powers of LEAs in the organization and delivery of education. We see this as the key to understanding the Thatcher government's educational and social policy programme and it has been important to emphasize this for two reasons. First, it provides clues to the rationale underpinning the apparently contradictory trajectories of the ERA; namely, the move towards greater centralization, on the one hand, and the devolution of responsibility and power, on the other. Both impulses cohere around a determined opposition to the 'state monopoly' of education which is overseen, in Baker's words, by 'hostile authorities' (Baker 1987: 7). Thus, the ERA establishes a reconstituted relationship between the traditional decision- and policy-making partnership in education. Here, the LEAs operate as mere functionaries of the centre; parental 'choice' and 'freedom' takes place in an arena in which financial and administrative arrangements are non-negotiable, having been prepared by and imposed from the centre.

Our concern about the future of LEAs under the ERA is important for another reason. In the continued absence of an explicit, national education policy on race-related matters (Dorn and Troyna 1982), the campaign for the promotion and legitimation of anti-racist education has taken place, with varying degrees of success, at the local level. Prior to the ERA, LEAs had the power, legitimacy and, as Robin Richardson (1988) reminds us, 'moral authority' to encourage local schools and colleges to take up the educational policies that were fomulated at their county halls. Needless to say, not all LEAs formulated policies on 'race' and of those that did a significant number decided not to use their powers to ensure the effective diffusion of the policies throughout the locality. The point that we want to stress, however, is this: the ERA presages a more diverse and fragmented school system in which the processes of 'opting out' and open enrolment and the local management of schools (LMS) scheme relocate the power of LEAs into the hands of individual governing bodies. In particular, these bodies will be responsible for overseeing the curriculum, testing and discipline; controlling the school budget; admissions policies; and the appointment, promotion and dismissal of staff. In this context, the achievements that were secured at LEA level in the 1980s are now obsolete and irrelevant. The terrain has changed; the struggle for the promotion and infusion of anti-racism into education provision and practices must now take place at the meetings of every school governing body. In the absence of the regulatory functions of the LEA, each governing body will need to be convinced of the value and efficacy of anti-racist education (and other egalitarian reforms) and be persuaded to use part of its restricted school budget to support existing (or develop new) initiatives along anti-racist lines. As we have made clear, neither the economic nor political climate seems conducive to such a development.

Baker's insistence that the ERA in general and the National Curriculum in particular 'will be very helpful in holding together a multi-racial and multi-cultural society' (*Guardian*, 17 August 1988) has a hollow ring to it. It contrasts starkly with the views of Baroness Hooper, the government's spokesperson in the House of Lords, who maintained that parent choice should not be curtailed by considerations of 'race' in the operation of open enrolment. Despite the argument that open enrolment might encourage 'white flight' and artificially create racially segregated schools, Baroness Hooper was adamant that, 'in giving parents choice, we do not wish to circumscribe that choice in any way' (*The Times Educational Supplement*, 13 May 1988). The systemic changes which the ERA mobilizes seem incompatible with anti-racist imperatives but what of the 'entitlement curriculum'?

Discussion points

1 What distinction would you make between political education and political indoctrination?

2 Max Morris and Clive Griggs see the ERA as 'loosening the bonds of local authority control of schools and their pupils' (1988). What are the likely consequences of this development for anti-racist and multicultural education?

5 The 'entitlement curriculum'?

If the Swann report can be desribed as a 'landmark in pluralism', then the ERA – with its silence on issues relating to 'race' and its stress on Christianity – may be regarded as signalling a return to a 'colour-blind' perspective. As Sally Tomlinson has remarked:

> The Education Reform Act became law in July 1988 and, despite the presence in the education system of over half a million children and young people perceived as racially or ethnically different to a white norm, there was no mention in the Act of race, ethnicity or even multicultural education.
>
> (Tomlinson 1989: 461)

In view of these and other 'silences' it is not surprising that many of the Act's critics fear that it will have a stifling effect on egalitarian policies in schools. Richard Johnson, for instance, has contended that not only does the legislation threaten 'to freeze educational development in a particular mould' but also that the National Curriculum is 'the nearest thing to the Government's own curriculum . . . with its endorsement of traditional subject boundaries, its neglect of interdisciplinarity, its insistence on "objective" forms of testing, and its closure on experimentation' (Johnson 1989: 117–18). The general secretary of the National Association of Headteachers, David Hart, has echoed these speculations, though from a polar standpoint. Addressing the association's annual conference in June 1989, he told delegates: 'The challenges of the 1990s will tolerate no egalitarianism and no anti-competitive attitude' (*Guardian*, 2 June 1989).

Despite the government's hostility towards egalitarian

policies, the National Curriculum is likely to offer some opportunities for anti-racist and multicultural initiatives. In this chapter, we plan to highlight these opportunities, as well as drawing attention to the constraints upon innovation in this sphere. In order to evaluate the plethora of policy and discussion documents that are currently emerging from the National Curriculum Council and the DES, we begin by briefly outlining a number of principles which might inform teaching about racism. We then move on to specify the main proposals for the National Curriculum and assess and evaluate the emerging policies from an anti-racist perspective.

Teaching about racism: some underlying principles

In Chapter 3, we made a case for teaching about racism in all primary and secondary schools, irrespective of ethnic composition or locality. We described the various forms taken by racist 'logic' and we provided examples to show how racism can inform 'many day-to-day judgements and, in turn, actions' (Cashmore 1987: 3). We claimed that, if teachers are to engage effectively with this 'logic', then consideration will need to be given to the medium as well as its message when devising curricular interventions. Let us now consider this argument in more detail.

As we have indicated elsewhere (e.g. Carrington and Troyna 1988; Carrington and Short 1987, 1989; Troyna 1987), curricular initiatives to combat racism should form part of a wider programme of political education which seeks, first, to develop young people's understanding of fundamental issues relating to human rights, social justice and the exercise of power and, second, to extend participation in the democratic process by equipping them with a range of skills and dispositions which they need to become decent, fair-minded, responsible and informed citizens. This approach, which attaches high priority to the goals of political and moral autonomy, encourages pupils to question their own and others' taken-for-granted beliefs and assumptions about social reality; to become informed sceptics who are able to take a critical stance towards ideological information; to give reasons for a point of view; to be open-minded and show respect for evidence; and to act with empathy and humanitarianism. As such, political education may provide not only a basis for the examination of racial inequality and discrimination but also a context for challenging racist stereotypes and myths. You will therefore see a marked resemblance between our view of political education and that of Robert Dunn (1984) and the Swann committee (DES 1985a), which we outlined in Chapter 4.

When devising anti-racist initiatives, particular attention must be given to the structure of classroom relationships and to teaching and learning styles. An authoritarian environment, where the teacher dominates 'official' classroom talk and where pupils lack either the confidence or the opportunity to express their own views, is markedly at variance with the principles and goals outlined above. As well as stressing the importance of a democratic ethos in classrooms and underlining the need for strategies to promote discussion, we should also like to stress the importance of teaching strategies which seek to develop co-operative skills. The evidence on co-operative (or collaborative) learning suggests that working together in pursuit of a common objective not only serves to enhance pupils' social awareness and their interpersonal and ethical skills but also does so without any apparent adverse effect on their level of attainment. In fact, under certain conditions, attainment levels may actually improve (Yeomans 1983). The technique has been successfully employed in multi-ethnic settings to ease intergroup conflicts and tensions. As Edith King's résumé of research has shown:

> In a school that has a single-minded concern with academic performance so that student is pitted against student in a competitive arena, very different lessons are being taught. Schools that are successful in developing prejudice reduction are ones in which minority and majority students come together as cooperating equals.
>
> (King 1986: 334)

King's observations will be borne in mind as we examine the implications of the emerging National Curriculum and its assessment for anti-racist and multicultural initiatives.

The National Curriculum

The Education Reform Act, as the DES Circular 5/89 reminds us, entitles every pupil in maintained schools to a curriculum 'which is balanced and broadly-based', and which:

(a) promotes the spiritual, moral, cultural, mental and physical development of pupils at the school and of society; and

(b) prepares such pupils for the opportunities, responsibilities and experiences of adult life.

(DES 1989b: para. 16)

The circular then proceeds to offer muted support for pluralism: 'It is intended that the curriculum should reflect the culturally diverse society to which pupils belong and of which they will become adult members' (DES 1989b: para. 17).

The National Curriculum, which has been introduced progressively since Autumn 1989, comprises three 'core' subjects (English, mathematics and science) and seven other 'foundation' subjects (technology, history, geography, music, art, physical education and, for all pupils aged 11–16, a modern language).

Although religious education (RE) remains a statutory requirement for all pupils in county and voluntary schools (unless their parents request otherwise), it is described as a 'basic' subject in the legislation and not included in the National Curriculum. In contrast to the foundation subjects, RE is not subject to nationally prescribed attainment targets, programmes of study and assessment arrangements (DES 1989a: para. 20).

While the 'foundation' subjects, together with RE, 'must figure in every pupil's curriculum to ensure delivery of his or her entitlement' (DES 1989c: para. 2.3), no fixed amount of time has been prescribed for studying these subjects. Notwithstanding this, it is generally recognized that at least 80 per cent of the school timetable will be given over to the National Curriculum. It is not only the Centre and Left who have argued that this could impose a strait-jacket on school staffs. Stuart Sexton, a leading figure on the New Right, has argued that:

By covering about 85% of the school timetable, the National Curriculum effectively removes from the options open to a child at any school many other highly desirable subjects

(Sexton 1988: 237).

However, we should like to point out that the DES has now acknowledged in its guidelines, *National Curriculum: From Policy to Practice* that the foundation subjects cannot be regarded as a complete curriculum:

> The *whole* curriculum for *all* pupils certainly needs to include at appropriate (and in some cases all) stages: careers education and guidance; health education; other aspects of personal and social education; and coverage across the curriculum of gender and multicultural issues.
>
> (DES 1989c: para. 3.8; original emphasis)

The document then goes on to endorse other cross-curricular issues which the New Right has disparaged as 'soft subjects', such as 'economic awareness, political and international understanding and environmental education' (DES 1989c: para. 3.9).

Assessment and testing

Whereas the government's proposals for the curriculum offer some possibilities for innovation along anti-racist and multicultural lines, its requirements for assessment and testing may serve to discourage experimentation in this sphere. The ERA makes provision for children to be tested in the foundation subjects at 7, 11, 14 and 16. Attainment targets will be set 'to establish what children should normally be expected to know, understand and be able to do' at these ages and the targets 'will enable the progress of each child to be measured against national standards' (DES 1989c: para. 6.4). Under the Act, schools will be required not only to provide parents with information about their own children's performance but also to publish the aggregated results of assessments at 11, 14 and 16. Although the DES 'strongly recommends' schools to publish the results for 7-year olds, this is not compulsory under the legislation. The DES has emphasized that 'LEAs will not be required to publish "league tables" for schools in their area' (DES 1989c: para. 7.4) but we believe that the policy will, nevertheless, encourage such practices, whether or not they are officially sanctioned.

The government's policy on testing is likely to have far-reaching consequences, especially for the primary school. As a result of pressures from parents and governors to achieve better test results, some schools may opt to teach children in classes which are determined by the children's ability rather than their age. Furthermore, there are indications that the DES would be prepared to sanction such a potentially divisive development (*Guardian*, 14 April 1989). The implications for anti-racist and multicultural education are considerable. If the advent of national testing does lead to the re-introduction of streaming in primary schools, then it is likely that many children of Afro-Caribbean origin could find themselves wrongly allocated to the lower streams (see Chapter 2). Although the DES (1988a: paras 51–2) has drawn attention to the dangers of cultural bias in testing, this is unlikely to obviate entirely the possibility that the tests themselves – or 'standardised assessment tasks' (SATS) – might discriminate against black children, particularly those with first languages other than English. The proposals for assessment and testing may also undermine initiatives to promote racial equality in other ways. With national testing, the ethic of competitive individualism, which is already prevalent in our schools, is likely to assume even great prominence. The increased emphasis on academic achievement could inhibit staff from experimenting with more democratic styles of teaching and learning, such as collaborative groupwork and other pedagogical strategies which are conducive to our vision of anti-racist education (Carrington and Short 1989: 160).

The requirements that are laid out in the ERA for religious education and daily acts of worship can also be seen as anathema to anti-racist and multicultural initiatives. Let us examine these requirements more closely before moving on to consider emerging policies in other areas of the curriculum.

Religious education and acts of worship

In Chapter 1, we argued that the New Right's specious conception of British culture as monolithic and ethnically undifferentiated and its concomitant characterization of black people as an 'alien wedge' have served to rationalize the exclusion of Afro-Caribbeans and South Asians from equal participation in social institutions. The sections of the Education Reform Act that deal with religious education and acts of worship in school are clearly imbued with such thinking. As John Hull, in an editorial of the *British Journal of Religious Education*, has pointed out: 'the most important feature of the new act as far as religion is concerned is the fact that for the first time Christianity is specifically mentioned' (Hull 1989: 119). Christianity, he claims, has been 'thrust into a position of embarrassing prominence'.

The legislation requires that any new syllabus in RE 'must reflect the fact that the religious traditions in the country are in the main Christian, while taking account of the teaching and practices of other principal religions' (Section 8:3), and that the daily act of collective worship in schools 'be wholly or mainly of a broadly Christian character' (Section 7:1). Not surprisingly, this part of the Act, with its avowedly assimilationist tenor, has provoked widespread criticism. Indeed, the National Association of Headteachers has predicted that the latter requirement will result in 'chaos' in schools (*Guardian*, 28 February 1989). The association claims that it will set schools on 'a collision course with some minority religions' and that some multi-faith schools not only do not have the staff to cope with supervising pupils who are excluded from mainly Christian assemblies, but also would be unable to provide alternative daily acts of worship in line with the legislation.

Hull, a staunch critic of the Act, has suggested that it may be possible for schools to find ways around the legislation. He argues that the phrase, '*mainly* of a broad Christian character' would enable schools to offer multi-faith assemblies comprising, for example: 'six verses from one of the Psalms, with five verses from the Qur'an, together with some simple prayers addressed to God' (Hull 1989: 121). He also claims that schools could meet the legal requirement if only three of the daily acts of worship during the course of a week were of 'a broad Christian character'.

While imaginative and sensitive staff will no doubt exploit such loopholes, this aspect of the legislation can serve only to undermine anti-racist and mutlicultural initiatives. The explicit emphasis on Christianity will probably lead to the withdrawal of many Muslims from RE lessons and assemblies

(Tomlinson 1989). Under the ERA, parents have the right not only to withdraw their children from these activities but also to request that the school makes alternative provision available (Section 9:4). Despite this, the Muslim Educational Trust is concerned that the statutory bodies who are responsible for dealing with such requests – the local Standing Advisory Councils on Religious Education (SACREs) – will be unlikely to act in an even-handed manner. The SACREs are composed of four groups representing, respectively:

(a) such Christian and other denominations as, in the opinion of the authority, will appropriately reflect the principal religious traditions in the area;
(b) the Church of England;
(c) such associations representing teachers as, in the opinion of the authority, ought to be represented, having regard to the circumstances of the area;
(d) the local education authority.

(Section 11:4)

Because Muslims would have only minority representation on a SACRE, the trust has argued that 'the bureaucrats could get the upper hand and we would be forced again to provide religious education for our children outside school and at our own expense' (*Guardian*, 28 Feburary 1989).

The statutory provisions for RE and assemblies are likely to heighten racial and ethnic divisions, both in schools and society at large. Immediately following the implementation of the Act two parents withdrew their children from a multi-ethnic primary school in Manchester because of their objection to its multi-faith assemblies and pluralist curriculum in RE. The parents sought a High Court ruling that their children be taught only Christianity at the school, in which 40 per cent of the pupils are of Asian origin. (Tomlinson 1989).

History

As well as thrusting Christianity into 'a position of embarrassing prominence', the New Right has also made strident demands for a more Anglocentric, patriotic approach to history teaching. Margaret Thatcher, her Education Secretary, John MacGregor, and his two predecessors, Kenneth Baker and Sir Keith Joseph, are all on record as wanting such an approach. 'One of the aims of teaching history', according to Joseph, 'is to understand the development of the shared values which are a distinctive feature of British culture and society' (cited in Arkell 1988: 30). Baker expressed a similar view when he informed the National Curriculum History Working Group that their proposals 'should have at the core the history of Britain, the record of its past and, in particular, its political, constitutional and cultural heritage' (DES 1989e: 15–16). MacGregor in response to the Working Group's interim report, said (on the advice of Thatcher) that he wanted 50 per cent more of the time devoted to British history in secondary schools, compared with just over a third envisaged for pupils aged 14–16. (*Observer*, 20 August 1989).

In the light of these declarations, it is not surprising that many commentators have voiced concern about the direction of history teaching in schools. For example, the distinguished historian Christopher Hill has shown how patriotic history tends to be jingoistic and 'sentimentally anecdotal'. He warns that: 'If we just go back to national self-glorification, to painting the map red, history will be in danger of becoming the plaything of party politics to be changed with a change of government' (Hill 1989: 9). In Hill's view, one of the aims of history should be to help us to 'come to grips with the horrors of our past'. Baker, however, refuses to acknowledge this view of British history. He told colleagues at the 1988 Conservative party conference that he was 'not ashamed of what we have done. Britian has given many great things to the world. That's been our civilising mission'. In contrast with Hill's 'warts and all' approach, pupils would not be encouraged to examine such topics as the long-term impact of slavery on the infrastructure of the West Indies, or the interrelationship between the slave trade, the colonization of the Caribbean and the rise of the UK as a major industrial nation and world power. Encouragement of such teaching would, of course, provide young people with an invaluable basis for understanding the development of racism in the UK.

Despite the restrictive terms of reference that were set for the History Working Group, chaired by Commander Michael Saunders, it eschewed patriotic history in its interim report. Saunders and his colleagues noted that, although British history was at the core of its proposals, 'it does not mean that it has to be at the centre of gravity' (DES 1989e: 18). As well as advocating a broadly-based curriculum comprising British history, European and world history and thematic studies, including local history, the Working Group distanced itself from the New Right's narrow conception of British culture by stressing that Britain and Ireland could not be perceived as 'an undifferentiated mass'. They noted that:

> Individual people in these islands have much in common but they also have many individual characteristics specific to country, ethnic grouping, religion, gender and social class. We do not believe that school history can be so finely tuned so as to accommodate all of these details all of the time, but at least it can make pupils aware of the richness and variety of British culture and its historical origins.
>
> (DES 1989e: 17)

While forgoing a monolithic view of British culture, the Working Party's liberal perspective nevertheless prompts it to view the nation as an essentially cohesive entity. Thus, class, racial and gender divisions are marginalized. As Saunders and his colleagues insist: 'the British dimension supplies the main framework of experience, in political, social, economic and cultural terms, within which pupils live now and are likely to live in the future' (DES 1989e: 16).

English

The Secretary of State's brief to the English Working Group, chaired by Brian Cox, was similarly Anglocentric:

> The Working Group's recommendations on learning about language and its use should draw upon the English literary heritage: should promote the reading of great literature and the knowledge and appreciation of literature; and should

indicate the types of literature which all pupils should cover in the course of their studies.

(Cited in Knight 1989: 53)

Despite this, the reports of the English Working Group (DES 1988d: 1989d) lend support to anti-racist and multicultural initiatives. No one would have predicted this outcome, especially from Professor Cox, one-time *bête noire* of progressive education and co-editor of the right-wing *Black Papers on Education*, which we mentioned in Chapter 4. Many expected Cox to endorse the traditionalist approach to the teaching of English that is favoured by Baker, Thatcher and the New Right. However, traditionalists have been largely disappointed by the Working Group's final recommendations, which were greeted by headlines such as 'Baker Accepts Defeat on Teaching of Grammar' (*Guardian*, 23 June 1989) and 'Rote Set to be Written out of the Syllabus' (*The Times Educational Supplement*, 30 June 1989).

Building on the recommendations of the Swann report (DES 1985a), Cox and his colleagues underline the need for a pluralist approach to the curriculum. They state that 'the curriculum for all pupils should include informed discussion of the multicultural nature of British society, whether or not the school is culturally mixed' (DES 1988d: para. 3.7). Particular attention is given by the Working Group to the issues that are raised by linguistic diversity, which it stresses should be seen as 'an enormous resource'. Drawing on the work of Viv Edwards (1979), Cox and his colleagues focus on the needs of bidialectal children, including those of Afro-Caribbean origin. (Bidialectalism refers to the ability to move from one variety of speech to another, e.g., from Black English, Scouse or Geordie to Standard English.) Although arguing that 'schools have a clear responsibility to ensure that all children have access to Standard English', the Working Group emphasizes that 'schools should teach in ways which do not denigrate the non-standard dialects spoken by many children' (DES 1988d: para. 4.24). Conscious of the relationship between language and social identity, Cox and his colleagues warn teachers against constantly criticizing and 'correcting' pupils' spoken language; such criticism is often interpreted by pupils as a rejection of their culture and values. The Working Group noted that Standard English cannot be regarded as 'inherently superior' to other dialects of English, even though 'it clearly has social prestige' (DES 1988d: para. 5.44).

In their first report, *English for Ages 5 to 11*, Cox and his colleagues recommended that children should study literature which is drawn from many different countries: 'Children need to be aware of the richness of contemporary writing, so that they might be introduced to the ideas and feelings of people from cultures different from their own' (DES 1988b: para. 6.3). On these grounds, the Working Group provided an illustrative list of more than two hundred authors, whose work might be used in primary school. The list, which includes Roald Dahl, Hugh Lofting, Bernard Ashley and Reverend W. Awdry, has attracted considerable criticism. Dawn Gill, for example, has drawn attention to the racist imagery that is so prevalent in Dahl's *Charlie and the Chocolate Factory*. She states:

> Dahl's books may be brilliantly entertaining, but the Cox Committee should be concerning themselves with the hidden curriculum in works of fiction and asking whether that in *Charlie and the Chocolate Factory* deserves to be uncritically imparted in schools.
>
> (Gill 1989: 37)

Similar criticisms can, of course, be levelled against some of the other authors who are mentioned in the report. Reverend Awdry's *Railway Series*, which features Thomas the Tank Engine and his Friends, has been shown to celebrate social hierarchies of class and gender, and to embody an ideology which shares many of the characteristis of Thatcherism (Carrington and Denscombe 1987)! Despite this, Cox's list is very much a 'mixed-bag'. While Lofting's *Dr Dolittle* may be criticized for imparting 'imperialist values' (Gill 1989), Ashley's novel, *The Trouble with Donovan Croft*, with its non-tokenistic treatment of black characters and realistic portrayal of social relationships in the primary school, may provide a useful basis for an anti-racist intervention (see Carrington and Short 1989: 106–14). Because of the controversy surrounding the publication of their list of authors, Cox and his colleagues decided not to include it in their final report.

We wholly endorse this decision because it is sometimes impossible for a teacher to make any definitive judgement about which book is suitable for use in the classroom and which is not. After all, a book that reinforces popular myths and stereotypes about 'race' or gender could provide a useful starting point for a group discussion about these issues. As Gillian Klein has argued: 'teachers can use *any* materials in the classroom including the overtly racist and sexist, as long as they are sensitive to the messages, and can challenge them as they arise' (Klein 1985: 174). Obviously, if children are to be encouraged to express and develop their own ideas about such issues in a sustained way, then particular attention will need to be given to the development of their oral skills. This is recognized by Cox and his colleagues, who attach considerable importance to the role of talk in promoting pupils' understanding. As Ian Nash has noted, when commenting on the emphasis that is given to oracy in *English for Ages 5 to 16*, 'the rise in status of the spoken word and the demotion of the written essay' could have 'a dramatic effect on the shape of English lessons' (Nash 1989: 8). It may encourage staff to experiment with more democratic forms of pedagogy. As we have pointed out earlier, such a shift, if it occurred, would be conducive to anti-racist initiatives.

Modern languages

As the English Working Group has acknowledged, a significant proportion of children attending urban schools in the UK are either bilingual or multilingual. It has been estimated that, in the ILEA alone, one in six children speak English as their second language and over 157 languages are spoke by pupils attending the authority's schools (see Kite 1988: 42). In many other urban centres, these proportions are either comparable or higher (Linguistic Minorities Project 1985: 336). Although ethnic minority languages will qualify as 'foundation subjects' in the National Curriculum, the government's draft order for language teaching fails to provide unequivocal support for Cox's view of linguistic diversity as 'an enormous resource'. As the

Commission for Racial Equality has pointed out, the draft order's division of languages into two schedules – European Community languages (schedule 1) and ethnic minority languages (schedule 2) – could lead to the mistaken assumption that pupils may only take an ethnic minority language if a European language is already being studied (CRE 1989). Moreover, it could also lead to ethnic minority languages being seen as having lower status than European ones.

Science and mathematics

In contrast to the draft order for language teaching, the proposals of the National Curriculum Working Groups in Science and Mathematics seem to be more sensitive to the issue of ethnocentricism. The Science Working Group, for instance, has emphasized that

> the science curriculum must provide opportunities to help all pupils recognise that no one culture has a monopoly of scientific achievement – for example through discussion of the origins and growth of chemistry from ancient Egypt and Greece to Islamic, Byzantine and European cultures, and parallel developments in China and India.
>
> (DES 1988b: para. 7.16)

Similarly, the Mathematics Working Group has argued that

> it will be important within the broad framework of National Curriculum attainment targets and programmes of study, to select examples and materials which relate to the cultural backgrounds of pupils. Some attention to the history of mathematics could show the contribution to the development of mathematical thinking of non-European cultures: for example, it would be right to point out that the number system is of Hindu–Arabic origin.
>
> (DES 1988c: para. 10.21)

Despite this, the Working Group is critical of what it describes as a 'multicultural approach to mathematics', with children being introduced to different number systems, foreign currencies and non-European measuring and counting devices'. As well as contending that 'undue emphasis' on these issues could confuse young children, the Working Group also endorses the critique of multiculturalism that is outlined by Troyna elsewhere (e.g. Troyna and Williams 1986: 45–59). In the view of the Working Group, the claim that a multicultural approach to mathematics 'is necessary to raise the self-esteem of ethnic minority cultures and to improve mutual understanding and respect between races' is both 'misconceived and patronising' (DES 1988c: para. 10.22). We agree.

It seems, therefore, that the policies emerging alongside the National Curriculum are rather like the Curate's egg: good in parts. On the positive side, the recommendations of the English Working Group would seem to offer some scope for anti-racist teaching. The DES has also lent its support to 'the coverage across the curriculum of gender and multicultural issues'. Moreover, it has acknowledged the need for cross-curricular teaching beyond the statutory National Curriculum in areas such as personal and social education and 'political and international understanding'. On the negative side, the basis of anti-racist conceptions of reform is undermined by the emphasis on Christianity in RE lessons and in school assemblies and, if Margaret Thatcher, John MacGregor and Kenneth Baker have their way, on patriotism in history. We have also shown how the new testing and assessment procedures could jeopardize such reforms by creating an ethos of intense competition within and between schools. Faced with pressures from parents and governors to produce 'good' results, many teachers will feel compelled to play safe by narrowly interpreting the government's programmes of study and gearing their lessons towards the Standard Assessment Tasks.

With the centralization of educational decision-making, we have witnessed a correlative decline in the power of the LEAs and schools to shape the development of the curriculum in any fundamental way. Prior to the ERA, there was a greater likelihood that LEAs might encourage local schools to unite in their efforts to promote equal opportunities and other progressive innovations. However, as the Chief Education Officer of Walsall, Dinah Tuck, informs us, this scenario has now changed:

the role of the LEA to look after the needs of all children it serves seems to be endangered if we perceive of each school as a private company competing rather than collaborating with its neighbours, not least when resources are limited.

(Tuck 1988: 148)

Discussion points

1 To what extent are the proposals for assessment and testing in schools compatible with the principles of ARE?
2 The National Association of Headteachers (NAHT) sees the requirement for school assemblies to be 'wholly or mainly of a broadly Christian character' as a recipe for chaos. In what ways do you think the anticipated chaos might be avoided?

6 Anti-racism in the new ERA

Room for manoeuvre

Anti-racist education is not 'flavour of the month'. On the contrary, it has been assailed from all quarters. It has been disparaged, misrepresented and parodied by the media, especially the tabloid press; dismissed by the New Right as a Marxian-inspired form of authoritarianism; castigated by Thatcherites as an irrelevant 'soft subject' which is inimical to 'good' educational practice; and criticized by a growing number of academics who prefer to nail their colours to the mast of cultural pluralism. The Education Reform Act 1988 largely sanctions these criticisms of ARE. For instance, the government's policies on religious education herald a return to assimilationism and promote a conception of the role of the school in a multi-racial society which is entirely compatible with the New Right's restricted view of British culture, heritage and citizenship. Similarly, the policy on modern languages accords higher status to European Community languages than to the main ethnic minority community languages. Again, the message is clear: second-class status for 'second class citizens'.

However, we see the weakening of the LEA powers which has accompanied centralization as having the most serious implications for the promotion of ARE and other egalitarian policies. We have shown that, during the 1980s, local authorities, especially those which have been Labour controlled, have been at the forefront of the campaign for racial equality. The reduction of LEA powers to influence the policies of its schools will allow individual headteachers and their governors, who may be sceptical of ARE, to adopt a 'colour blind' perspective.

The ramifications of this shift towards assimilationism are far-reaching, especially in all-white/non-contact areas such as Cumbria, Devon and the north east of England. There, nascent support for ARE is likely to be drastically curtailed. Naturally, the government was not unaware of this possibility when it drafted its provisions for the local management of schools and for 'opting out'. As Stuart Maclure has noted, these provide alternatives

> for parents in areas where political extremists had gained control over the local education authority. . . . The new type of school was to be seen as a means by which parents could place the education of their children beyond the reach of the local education authority and its policy on, say, . . . racism, and gender issues.
>
> (Maclure 1988: 64)

Despite this onslaught, we have retained our commitment to ARE. Why? Because, as we have argued elsewhere, 'ARE constitutes an emancipatory notion of educational change which embraces styles of teaching and classroom organisation that have the potential to facilitate the cognitive, social and affective development of children' (Carrington and Troyna 1988: 211). These principles are, of course, congruent with good practice.

We began this book by drawing attention to Stuart Hall's claim that social science is about 'deconstructing the obvious' and subjecting to critical scrutiny taken-for-granted assumptions about social reality. One of these assumptions was captured in Kenneth Baker's assertion that the ERA would 'open the doors of opportunity [not] slam them in front of our children'. We are told by the DES that these 'doors' are opened by a curriculum which is 'balanced and broadly based' and which prepares young people for 'the responsibilities and experiences of adult life'. But are they? To achieve these goals, schools will need to pay as much attention to the development of children's political knowledge and awareness as they do to their 'spiritual, moral, cultural, mental and physical development'. Although there are no statutory provisions for the National Curriculum to develop political literacy, we saw in Chapter 5 that the DES document, *National Curriculum: From Policy to Practice*, does identify 'economic awareness, political and international understanding and environmental education' as integral elements of a 'complete' curriculum. Moreover, whilst we anticipate that the government's prescriptions for curriculum *content* will impact directly (and negatively) on pedagogy, we are not entirely in disagreement with Tony Jeffs's view that: 'Despondency need not be the order of the day'. He reckons that the 'hidden' or informal curriculum, over which teachers will continue to have a large say, plays an important part in structuring pupils' political perspectives. Jeffs states that:

> it is essential not to overestimate the curriculum and the timetable since, in relation to matters of belief, attitude and values, the wider context of the school organization and the pattern of classroom control are far more influential than the content of the lessons.

> (Jeffs 1988: 47)

Certainly the translation of TVEI policy into practice seems to support Jeffs's cautiously optimistic view of the post-ERA phase. TVEI was introduced to enhance the skills and dispositions which young people were said to require for the world of work. However, as Denis Gleeson writes in *The Paradox of Training* (1989), the 'content and form of technical and vocational education remains contested rather than given' and there is evidence of teachers appropriating TVEI for the purpose of initiating and supporting egalitarian reforms in pedagogy (Gleeson 1989: 89). There is, therefore, some room for manoeuvre. With this in mind, let us now look at ways in which different models of political education may be used to address the issue of racial inequality in schools and colleges.

Political education and ARE

Children's first-hand knowledge of 'race' relations will invariably provide the starting-point for such a programme in the multi-ethnic primary school. From the standpoint that anti-racist teaching is best undertaken in an environment where a frank and open exchange of ideas is encouraged, Martin Francis (1984) has described an intervention with fourth year juniors, which began with a class discussion of racial incidents at their school. This initial discussion was to provide the basis for a wide-ranging, cross-curriculum project, which dealt with various facets of racial inequality, both in the UK and abroad.

Clearly, teachers who are implementing an anti-racist initiative in 'non-contact' areas are unable to draw upon the children's direct knowledge in this way. When broaching the issue of 'race' in the classroom, they often have no other option than to rely on secondary sources (e.g. black autobiographical accounts, newspaper articles, photographs, census materials) or fantasy (role play, fiction) as stimuli. It was this difficulty that confronted Short and Carrington (1987) when they devised their integrated project (*In Living Memory*) for use with 10–11 year olds in an 'all-white' primary school. The project was concerned with changes in popular culture and lifestyle since the Second World War. It began with the immediate experiences of the children and members of their family. The children interviewed their parents and grandparents about their employment histories and work experiences and their perceptions of cultural change in a variety of spheres. These oral histories, together with artefacts such as family photographs, memorabilia and local archive materials, provided a starting-point for a study which extended beyond the local environment. A class discussion of recent historical changes in the demand for labour in the UK not only permitted the issues of 'race' and immigration to arise spontaneously but also provided an appropriate context for exploring the 'logic' of racism, including racial stereotyping and scapegoating. Various techniques were used to encourage members of the class to empathize with black people. For example, the children were asked to place themselves in the position of an Afro-Caribbean or South Asian migrant worker in the 1950s; in this capacity, they were invited to write to a relative or friend describing their experiences in the UK. These 'letters' were then compared with black autobiographical accounts of the period. To sharpen the children's awareness of how contemporary racism influences the lives of British-born Afro-Caribbean and South Asians, various teaching strategies were deployed. These included the use of children's literature, role-play activities and group discussion.

Subsequently a modified version of the project was used with children aged 11–13 in an all-white middle school (Carrington and Short 1989: 106–14). Throughout this and the previous intervention, extensive use was made of collaborative group work and other methods to democratize the classroom and to facilitate open discussion.

As we have already indicated when discussing the contact hypothesis, the idea of 'ethnic proximity as a recipe for racial harmony' should not be exaggerated. Despite this, it is often argued that the success of an anti-racist initiative is dependent on pupils having *direct* experience of other ethnic groups. But does it? Let us look at two projects which have operated this principle. These involved, first, an exchange between a multi-ethnic and 'all-white' primary school (Lee *et al.* 1987) and, second, an anti-racist intervention with a fourth year English class in a Walsall secondary school (Hatcher 1988).

Veronica Lee and her colleagues brought together two junior classes at Park School (a multi-ethnic, inner-city school) and Riverside School (an all-white suburban school). Mutual visits were arranged because both class teachers felt that these would provide the children with an opportunity 'to share and explore each other's social perspectives, particularly those relating to race' (Lee *et al.* 1987: 209). Before the visits took place, each teacher undertook a considerable amount of preparatory work with their class on stereotyping (by 'race' and gender), racist name-calling, and forms of bias in the media. As a follow-up to this work, the classes met on four occasions: the children from the inner-city school organized a Divali celebration to entertain their suburban peers. Later, they hosted an urban trail. Riverside also hosted a trail and arranged various problem-solving activities, involving collaboration between children from both schools. School exchanges such as these can reinforce, rather than undermine, racist conceptions of black people and their culture (Bochner 1982). However, Lee and her colleagues appeared to overcome this difficulty by incorporating the visits within a wider programme of political education and by selecting activities which stressed co-operation between the schools.

A similar strategy has been employed by Richard Hatcher

(1988) in his anti-racist intervention in the Midlands. Working with pupils who were drawn from a predominantly white secondary school in Walsall, Hatcher arranged a number of visits to Handsworth, 'an area with a large black community a few miles away in neighbouring Birmingham'. He found that many of the pupils had internalized negative images of Handsworth even though none had any 'direct personal experience' of the area. The project sought to provide this experience and the work that was undertaken comprised part of the language and literature components of the GCSE English syllabus. In order to engage with racist forms of 'logic', Hatcher and the pupils explored a number of aspects of life in Handsworth. Some groups studied the changing employment opportunities for black people in the area from the 1950s through to the present, while others 'dug out the facts behind the headlines', as they investigated crime and policing in Handsworth.

> They read Farrukh Dhondy's *The Seige of Babylon, Piggy in the Middle* by Jan Needle – a novel about racism in the police force – and poems by Linton Kwesi Johnson. Out of all this they began to make their own connections between crime, unemployment and racism.
>
> (Hatcher 1988: 19)

Others examined racist harassment and attacks in the Handsworth area and read Susan Price's novel, *From Where I Stand*, which deals with racism in a school setting. Some of this work was undertaken collaboratively with pupils from a Handsworth school.

Although the evaluation of the project revealed a generally positive shift in the pupils' attitudes to 'race', Hatcher continues to share our reservations about the contact hypothesis. He states:

> I am not saying that direct experiences of 'race' automatically leads to anti-racist learning. On the contrary, they can result in a reinforcing of racist attitudes. Popular racism is not the simple product of white ignorance which can be overcome by

positive experiences of 'black culture' or of 'inter-ethnic contact'.

(Hatcher 1988: 23)

Based in the post–16 sector, Troyna and Selman's (1989) action research in an 'all-white' college of further education provides another framework for intervention along anti-racist lines. In theoretical terms, their aim was to alert white students, through political education, to the complex social and racial formation of the state. Here, 'race' is interconnected with class and gender divisions as constitutive elements in the maintenance of hegemonic domination. As Troyna argues, this sophisticated understanding of how social, political and historical processes of society have institutionalized power cannot be broached by tackling racial inequality in isolation. Thus:

Rather than imposing the burden of racial inequality on white youngsters (*qua* white youngsters) the aim of ARE must be to encourage them to recognise not only the specific nature of racial discourse and practice but the forms of inequality they themselves experience and share with black people: as women, young people, residents in an economically depressed area of the UK or as members of the working class. To distil commonalities within a framework where differences are recognized.

(Troyna 1989: 184)

The implementation of this broadly conceived interpretation of inequality proceeded through the identification of core concepts, including 'bias' and 'rights'. Around these, Troyna and Selman (1989) organized teaching sessions, co-operated with students in the production of materials and collaborated with them, in a relatively non-competitive environment, in teasing out horizontal (rather than vertical) connections in the exploration and understanding of inequality and oppression. Whilst the project was not subject to either formal or rigorous evaluation, there is evidence to suggest that its presence in the college helped to stimulate a move away from its traditional commitment to 'colour blind' ways of operating. This brief, episodic intervention into the life of the students and college led, in part, to the reappraisal of the library stock, the establishment of staff development programmes and the formulation of equal opportunities policies for both the Students' Union and the college in general.

This determination to identify and make links between the different forms of oppression and inequality which are experienced directly by members of the school (or college) community, including pupils, teachers, parents and governors, suggests a possible direction for anti-racism in the wake of the Education Reform Act. By alerting these members to the way in which institutionalized inequality might have influenced their own life-chances, as black people, women, young people, working-class or unemployed citizens, we might be in a better position to mobilize support for campaigns which are geared towards tackling racial inequality within more broadly conceived equal opportunities initiatives.

Mobilizing support

Obviously, such programmes can proceed only with the full support of parents and governors. With the ERA and its proposals for LMS, it is essential that both 'the producers' and 'the consumers' are convinced of the positive contribution that ARE can make to the educational experiences of pupils. Put another way, the school community, conceived in its fullest sense, must be discouraged from viewing ARE as a 'frill', 'irrelevant fad' or subterfuge for indoctrination. Staff will also have to demonstrate that ARE interventions do not detract from any of the academic (or other) goals that are laid out in the National Curriculum. We have shown in this book that Mrs Thatcher is not alone in characterizing ARE as synonymous with the lowering of academic standards. Thus a logical extension of our argument is that the managerial and professional autonomy which, in some institutions, tended to accompany ARE initiatives in the mid–1980s must be eschewed in favour of a more democratized approach to the planning, implementation and evaluation of such programmes. There are already established precedents for the involvement of parents and governors in these processes, as we have shown before

(Carrington and Troyna 1988). In short, we see a whole school approach, in which the community in its entirety is an active participant, as essential to the development of ARE. Does this sound idealistic? Perhaps it is. After all, even before the onslaught of the anti-anti-racists and the proliferation of (often fraudulent) accounts of over-zealous ARE campaigns, teachers in one LEA were voicing strong opposition to the authority's calls for anti-racist and multicultural education reforms. The reason was that some saw these orthodoxies as divisive, others as peripheral to their concerns in a period of educational contraction (Troyna and Ball 1985). Similarly, it would be foolhardy to believe that all parents would support the move towards ARE in their local school. Support has to be won rather than assumed as shown by events in Dewsbury and at Burnage High School in Manchester and by the results of an opinion poll for London Weekend Television in 1987 which found that more than 40 per cent of a sample of white parents in the south east of England favoured race-segregated schools. Nevertheless, it would also be politically inept to assume, *a priori*, community opposition to egalitarian reforms in education. To do so would be to ignore the findings of the British Social Attitudes survey which showed broad support for the development of multicultural education in schools (Jowell *et al.*. 1988: 26–7). It would also encourage acquiescence to Conservative interpretations of reality or, at best, the rejuvenation of the professional defensiveness and anti-democratic postures of the mid-1980s. With the Education Reform Act, the imperative for educational professionals must be to work in alliance with the wider community in the promotion of ARE and other egalitarian initiatives. The challenge of the 1990s will be to develop credible and effective strategies in order to realize this goal.

Discussion points

1 Anti-racist education is often depicted as an irrelevant fad which is inimical to 'good' educational practice. How would you justify teaching from an anti-racist perspective to school governors, parents and colleagues, who are sceptical of this approach?

2 The 'contact hypothesis' has a number of flaws. What conditions are necessary to ensure that school exchanges have a positive effect on pupils' racial attitudes?

References

Akhtar, S. and Stronach, I. (1986) 'They call me blacky', *The Times Educational Supplement* 19 September: 23.

All London Teachers Against Racism and Fascism (1979) *Racism in Schools*, London: ALTARF.

Apple, M. (1986) *Teachers and Texts*, London: Routledge & Kegan Paul.

Arkell, T. (1988) 'History's role in the school curriculum', *Journal of Education Policy* 3 (1): 23–38.

Bagley, C. (1970) *Social Structure and Prejudice in Five Boroughs*, London: Institute of Race Relations.

Baker, K. (1987) *Speech to Annual Conservative Party Conference*, Blackpool, 7 October.

Baker, K. (1988) *Speech to Annual Conservative Party Conference*, Brighton, 13 October.

Ball, W. and Troyna, B. (1989) 'The dawn of a new ERA? The Education Reform Act, "race" and LEAs', *Educational Management and Administration* 17 (2): 23–31.

Barker, M. (1981) *The New Racism*, London: Junction Books.

Barrow, J. *et al* (1986) 'The Two Kingdoms: Standards and Concerns, Parents and Schools: Independent Investigation into Secondary Schools in Brent 1981–1984', Unpublished, London: Brent Education Department.

Becker, H. (1952) 'Social class variations in the teacher–pupil relationships', *American Journal of Educational Sociology* 25 (4): 451–65.

Bennett, N. (1976) *Teaching Styles and Pupil Progress*, London: Open Books.

Bethnal Green and Stepney Trades Council (1978) *Blood on the Streets*, London: Bethnal Green and Stepney Trades Council.

Billig, M., Condor, S., Edwards, D., Gane, M., Middleton, D. and Radley, A. (1988) *Ideological Dilemmas: A Social Psychology of Everyday Thinking*, London: Sage.

Bochner, S. (1982) 'The social psychology of cross-cultural relations', pp. 5–44 in S. Bochner (ed.) *Cultures in Contact: Studies in Cross-Cultural Interaction*, London: Pergamon Press.

Brake, M. (1980) *The Sociology of Youth Culture and Youth Sub-Cultures*, London: Routledge & Kegan Paul.

Brandt, G. (1987) *The Realization of Anti-Racist Teaching*, Lewes: Falmer Press.

Brown, C. (1984) *Black and White Britain*, London: Policy Studies Institute/Heinemann.

Burgess, R.G. (1986) *Sociology, Education and Schools*, London: Batsford.

Callaghan, J. (1976) 'Speech', reprinted in *Education* 22 October: 332–3.

Carrington, B. (1983) 'Sport as a side-track. An analysis of West Indian involvement in extra-curricular sport', pp. 40–65 in L. Barton and S. Walker (eds) *Race, Class and Education*, Beckenham: Croom Helm.

Carrington, B. and Denscombe, M. (1987) 'Doubting Thomas: reading between the lines', *Children's Literature in Education* 18 (1): 45–53.

Carrington, B. and Short, G. (1987) 'Breakthrough to political literacy: political education, antiracist teaching and the primary school', *Journal of Education Policy* 2 (1): 1–13.

Carrington, B. and Short, G. (1989) *'Race' and the Primary School*, Windsor: NFER/Nelson.

Carrington, B. and Troyna, B. (1988) 'Combating racism through political education', pp. 205–23 in B. Carrington and B. Troyna (eds) *Children and Controversial Issues: Strategies for the Early and Middle Years of Schooling*, Lewes: Falmer Press.

Carrington, B., Millward, A. and Short, G. (1986) 'Schooling in a multiracial society: contrasting perspectives of primary and secondary teachers in training', *Educational Studies* 12 (1): 17–35.

Carter, B. and Williams, J. (1987) 'Attacking racism in education', pp. 170–83 in B. Troyna (ed.) *Racial Inequality in Education*, London: Tavistock.

Casey, J. (1982) 'One nation: the politics of race', *The Salisbury Review* Autumn: 23–8.

Cashmore, E. (1987) *The Logic of Racism*, London: Allen & Unwin.

Cashmore, E. (1988) 'Ethnicity', pp. 97–102 in E. Cashmore (ed.) *Dictionary of Race and Ethnic Relations: Second Edition*, London: Routledge.

Cashmore, E. and Troyna, B. (1990) *Introduction to Race Relations: Second Edition*, Lewes: Falmer Press.

Chevannes, M. and Reeves, F. (1987) 'The black voluntary school movement: definition, context and prospects', pp. 147–69 in B. Troyna (ed.) *Racial Inequality in Education*, London: Tavistock.

Chivers, T. (ed.) (1987) *Race and Culture in Education: Issues Arising from the Swann Committee Report*, Windsor: NFER/Nelson.

Coard, B. (1971) *How the West Indian Child is Made Educationally Sub-Normal in the British School System*, London: New Beacon Books.

Coffield, F., Borrill, C. and Marshall, S. (1986) *Growing up at the Margins,* Milton Keynes: Open University Press.

Cohen, P. (1988) 'The perversions of inheritance: studies in the making of multiracist Britain', pp. 1–123 in P. Cohen and H. Bains (eds) *Multi-racist Britain*, London: Macmillan.

Cole, M. (1989) ' "Whose is this country anyway? Who was here first?" An analysis of the attitudes of white first year B.Ed. students to immigration to Britain', *Multicultural Teaching* 7 (2): 15–17.

Commission for Racial Equality (1985) *Birmingham Local Education Authority and Schools: Referral and Suspension of Pupils*, London: CRE.

Commission for Racial Equality (1988) *Learning in Terror: a Survey of Racial Harassment in Schools and Colleges*, London: CRE.

Commission for Racial Equality (1989) *Press Release: CRE Responds to Government's Proposals on Modern Languages Teaching*, London, 27 April.

Cross, M. (1989) 'Contribution to "Race and Society" ', *New Statesman and Society* 7 April: 35.

Cullingford, C. (1984) 'The battle for the schools: attitudes of parents and teachers towards education', *Educational Studies* 10 (2): 113–19.

Dale, R. (1981) 'Schools, accountability and William Tyndale', pp. 305–18 in R. Dale, G. Esland, R. Fergusson and M. MacDonald (eds) *Education and the State: Vol. 2, Politics, Patriarchy and Practice*, Lewes: Falmer Press.

Davey, A. (1987) 'Interethnic friendship patterns in British schools over three decades', *New Community* 14 (1/2): 202–9.

Demaine, J. (1988) 'Teachers' work, curriculum and the New Right', *British Journal of Sociology of Education* 9 (3): 247–63.

DES (1977) *Education in Schools: A Consultative Document* (Green Paper) Cmnd 6869, London: HMSO.

DES (1981) *West Indian Children in Our Schools* (Interim report of the Committee of Inquiry into the Education of Children from Ethnic Minority Groups), Cmnd 8273, London: HMSO.

DES (1985a) *Education for All* (Final Report of the Committee of Inquiry into the Education of Children from Ethnic Minority Groups), Cmnd 9543, London: HMSO.

DES (1985b) *Better Schools* (White Paper), London: HMSO.

DES (1987) *Great Education Reform Bill* (White Paper), London: HMSO.

DES (1988a) *National Curriculum Task Group on Assessment and Testing: A Report*, London: HMSO.

DES (1988b) *Science for Ages 5 to 16*, London: HMSO.

DES (1988c) *Mathematics for Ages 5 to 16*, London: HMSO.

DES (1988d) *English for Ages 5 to 11*, London: HMSO.

DES (1989a) *The Education Reform Act 1988: Religious Education and Collective Worship, Circular No. 3/89*, London: HMSO.

DES (1989b) *The Education Reform Act 1988: The School Curriculum and Assessment, Circular No. 5/89*, London: HMSO.

DES (1989c) *National Curriculum: From Policy to Practice,*

London: HMSO.

DES (1989d) *English for Ages 5 to 16*, London: HMSO.

DES (1989e) *National Curriculum: History Working Group Interim Report*, London: HMSO.

Dhondy, F., Beese, B. and Hassan, L. (1982) *The Black Explosion in British Schools*, London: Race Today Publications.

Dorn, A. and Troyna, B. (1982) 'Multiracial education and the politics of decision-making', *Oxford Review of Education* 8 (2): 175–85.

Dunn, R. (1984) 'Speech', reprinted in *Teaching Politics* February: 295.

Edwards, V.K. (1979) *The West Indian Language Issue in British Schools*, London: Routledge & Kegan Paul.

Figueroa, P.M.E. (1984) 'Race relations and cultural difference: some ideas on a racial frame of reference', pp. 15–28 in G.K. Verma and C. Bagley (eds) *Race Relations and Cultural Differences*, Beckenham: Croom Helm.

Fisher, S. (1981) 'Race, class, anomie and academic achievement: a study at the High School level', *Urban Education* 16 (2): 149–73.

Focus Consultancy Limited (1988) 'Accepting the Challenge: The Report of a Consultation carried out with the Black and Ethnic Minority Communities of Hackney on the Transfer of Education to the London Borough of Hackney', Unpublished, London: Focus Consultancy Ltd.

Francis, M. (1984) 'Antiracist teaching in the primary school', pp. 34–42 in M. Straker-Welds (ed.) *Education for a Multicultural Society: Case Studies in ILEA Schools*, London: Bell & Hyman.

Furnham, A. and Gunter, B. (1989) *The Anatomy of Adolescence*, London: Routledge.

Gibson, M. (1976) 'Approaches to multicultural education in the United States: some concepts and assumptions', *Anthropology and Education Quarterly* 7 (4): 7–18.

Gill, D. (1989) 'National Curriculum: acceptable authors', *Multicultural Teaching* 7 (2): 36–7.

Gleeson, D. (1989) *The Paradox of Training*, Milton Keynes: Open University Press.

Gordon, P. and Rosenberg, D. (1989) *Daily Racism: The Press and Black People in Britain*, London: Runnymede Trust.

Green, P. (1982) 'Tolerance, teaching and the self-concept in the multi-ethnic classroom', *Multi-Ethnic Education* 1 (1): 8–11.

Gretton, J. and Jackson, M. (1976) *William Tyndale: Collapse of a School or a System?*, London: Allen & Unwin.

Gurnah, A. (1987) 'Gatekeepers and caretakers: Swann, Scarman and the social policy of containment', pp. 11–28 in B. Troyna (ed.) *Racial Inequality in Education*, London: Tavistock.

Gutmann, A. (1988) 'Democratic theory and the role of teachers in democratic education', *Journal of Education Policy* 3 (5): 183–99.

Hall, S. (1980) 'Teaching race', *Multiracial Education* 9 (1): 3–13.

Hargreaves, D.H. (1982) *The Challenge for the Comprehensive School: Culture, Curriculum and Community*, London: Routledge & Kegan Paul.

Hassan, L. and Beese, B. (1981) 'Who's educating whom?', pp. 21–35 in F. Dhondy, B. Beese and L Hassan (eds) *The Black Explosion in British Schools*, London: Race Today Publications.

Hatcher, R. (1987) 'Race and education: two perspectives for change', pp. 184–200 in B. Troyna (ed.) *Racial Inequality in Education*, London: Tavistock.

Hatcher, R. (1988) 'Antiracist learning: a local studies approach', *Multicultural Teaching* 7 (1): 19–24.

Henriques, J. (1984) 'Social psychology and the politics of racism', pp. 60–89 in J. Henriques, W. Holloway, C. Urwin, C. Venn and V. Walkerdine (ed.) *Changing the Subject: Psychology, Social Regulation and Subjectivity*, London: Methuen.

Her Majesty's Inspectorate (1987) *Educational Provision in the Outer London Borough of Brent*, London: HMSO.

Her Majesty's Inspectorate (1988) *The Development Programme for Race Equality in the London Borough of Brent*, London: HMSO.

Hill, C. (1989) 'Lies about crimes', *Guardian* 29 May: 9.

Hillgate Group (1987) *The Reform of British Education: From Principles to Practice*, London: Claridge Press.

Home Office (1981) *Racial Attacks*, London: HMSO.

Home Office (1989) *The Response to Racial Attacks and Harassment: Guidance for the Statutory Agencies*, London: HMSO.

Honeyford, R. (1988) *Integration or Disintegration? Towards a Non-Racist Society*, London: Claridge Press.

Horowitz, E.L. (1936) 'Development of attitudes towards negroes', pp. 111–21 in H. Proschansky and B. Seidenberg (eds) *Basic Studies in Social Psychology*, New York: Holt, Rinehart & Winston.

Hull, J. (1989) 'Editorial: school worship and the 1988 Education Reform Act', *British Journal of Religious Education* 11 (3): 119–25.

Hurd, D. (1989) 'Race relations and the rule of law', Speech presented at the Birmingham Central Mosque, 24 February.

Inner London Education Authority (1967) *The Education of Immigrants in Special Schools for ESN Children*, Report 657, London: ILEA.

Inner London Education Authority (1987) *Ethnic Background and Examination Results 1985 and 1986* (RS 1120/87), London: ILEA Research and Statistics Branch.

Inner London Education Authority (1988) *Suspension and Expulsions from School: 1986-7*, (RS1197/88), London: ILEA.

Jeffcoate, R. (1977) 'Children's racial ideas and feelings', *English in Education* 11 (1): 32–48.

Jeffcoate, R. (1979) *Positive Image: Towards a Multiracial Curriculum*, London: Chameleon Books/Readers and Writers Publishing Cooperative.

Jeffcoate, R. (1982) *The Education of Ethnic Minority Children in Britain, 1960-1980* (Open University E354), Milton Keynes: Open University.

Jeffcoate, R. (1984) *Ethnic Minorities and Education*, London: Harper & Row.

Jeffs, T. (1988) 'Preparing young people for participatory democracy', pp. 29–53 in B. Carrington and B. Troyna (eds) *Children and Controversial Issues: Strategies for the Early and Middle Years of Schooling*, Lewes: Falmer Press.

Jenkins, R. (1986) *Racism and Recruitment: Managers, Organ-*

isations and Equal Opportunity in the Labour Market, Cambridge: Cambridge University Press.

Johnson, R. (1989) 'Thatcherism and English education: breaking the mould, or confirming the pattern?', *History of Education* 18 (2): 91–121.

Joseph, Sir Keith (1986) 'Without prejudice: education for an ethnically mixed society', *New Community* XIII (2): 200–3.

Jowell, R., Witherspoon, S. and Brook, L. (1986) *British Social Attitudes: the 1986 Report*, Aldershot: Gower.

Jowell, R., Witherspoon, S. and Brook, L. (1988) *British Social Attitudes: the 5th Report*, Aldershot: Gower.

Killian, L. (1979) 'School bussing in Britain: policies and perceptions', *Harvard Educational Review* 49 (2): 185–206.

King, E. (1986) 'Recent experimental strategies for prejudice reduction in American schools and classrooms', *Journal of Curriculum Studies* 18 (3): 331–8.

Kirp, D. (1979) *Doing Good By Doing Little*, London: University of California Press.

Kite, U.R. (1988) 'Multilingualism and cultural exchange in Great Britain: with special reference to London schools', *British Journal of Language Teaching* 26 (1): 42–4.

Klein, G. (1985) *Reading into Racism: Bias in Children's Literature and Learning Materials*, London: Routledge & Kegan Paul.

Knight, H. (1989) 'The case for "multicultural literature" in the largely-white school', *English in Education* 23 (1): 51–5.

Lane, Sir David (1988) *Brent's Development Programme for Racial Equality in Schools: A Report*, London: Home Office.

Lasker, B. (1929) *Racial Attitudes in Children*, New York: Holt.

Lawrence, D. (1974) *Black Migrants, White Natives: a Study of Race Relations in Nottingham*, Cambridge: Cambridge University Press.

Lee, V., Lee, J. and Pearson, M. (1987) 'Stories children tell', pp. 207–19 in A. Pollard (ed.) *Children and their Primary Schools: a New Perspective*, Lewes: Falmer Press.

Leicester, M. (1989) 'Deconstructing anti anti-racist cognition', *Multicultural Teaching* 7 (2): 10–11.

Linguistic Minorities Project (1985) *The Other Languages of England*, London: Routledge & Kegan Paul.

Little, A. (1975) 'The educational achievement of ethnic minority children in London schools', pp. 48–69 in G.K. Verma and C. Bagley (eds) *Race and Education Across Cultures*, London: Heinemann Educational Books.

Lynch, J. (1987) *Prejudice Reduction and the Schools*, London: Cassell.

Mac an Ghaill, M. (1988) *Young, Gifted and Black*, Milton Keynes: Open University Press.

MacDonald, I., Bhavnani, R., Khan, L. and John, G. (1989) *Murder in the Playground*, London: Longsight Press.

Mack, J. (1977) 'As black as painted?', *New Society* 24 March: 589–90.

Maclure, S. (1988) *Education Re-formed*, London: Hodder & Stoughton.

Menter, I. (1987) 'Evaluating teacher education: some notes on an anti-racist programme for B.Ed. students', *Multicultural Teaching* 5 (3): 39–41.

Milner, D. (1983) *Children and Race: Ten Years On*, London: Ward Lock Educational.

Morris, M. and Griggs, C. (1988) 'Thirteen wasted years?', pp. 1–27 in M. Morris and C. Griggs (eds) *Education: The Wasted Years? 1973-1986*, Lewes: Falmer Press.

Mortimore, P., Sammons, P., Stoll, L., Lewis, D. and Ecob, R. (1988) *School Matters: The Junior Years*, Somerset: Open Books.

Mould, W. (1987) 'The Swann Report: an LEA response', pp. 44–60 in T. Chivers (ed.) *Race and Culture in Education*, Windsor: NFER/Nelson.

Mukherjee, T. (1988) 'The Journey Back', pp. 211–25 in P. Cohen and H.S. Bains (eds) *Multiracist Britain*, London: Macmillan.

Mullard, C. (1982) 'Multiracial education in Britain: from assimilation to cultural pluralism', pp. 120–33 in J. Tierney (ed.) *Race, Migration and Schooling*, London: Holt, Rinehart & Winston.

Mullard, C. (1984) *Anti-Racist Education: The Three O's*, Cardiff: National Antiracist Movement in Education.

Mullard, C. (1986) 'A critique of the Swann report', pp. 34–42 in G.K. Verma and D. Darby (eds) *Proceedings on the Swann*

Report, Bradford: University of Bradford.

Musgrove, F. (1987) 'The Black Paper movement', pp. 106–28 in R. Lowe (ed.) *The Changing Primary School*, Lewes: Falmer Press.

Nash, I. (1989) 'Rote set to be written out of the syllabus', *The Times Educational Supplement* 30 June: 8–9.

National Antiracist Movement in Education (1985) *NAME on Swann*, Nottingham: NAME.

National Union of Teachers (1989) *Anti-Racism in Education: Guidelines*, London: NUT.

Oldman, D. (1987) 'Plain-speaking and pseudo-science: the "New Right" attack on antiracism', pp. 29–43 in B. Troyna (ed.) *Racial Inequality in Education*, London: Tavistock.

Palmer, F. (ed.) (1986) *Anti-racism: an Assault on Education and Value*, London: Sherwood Press.

Parekh, B. (1983) 'Educational opportunity in multi-ethnic Britain', pp. 108–23 in N. Glazer and K. Young (eds) *Ethnic Pluralism and Public Policy*, London: Heinemann Educational Books.

Parekh, B. (1986) 'The concept of multicultural education', pp. 19–32 in S. Modgil, G.K. Verma, K. Mallick and C. Modgil (eds) *Multicultural Education: the Interminable Debate*, Lewes: Falmer Press.

Parekh, B. (1987) 'The education maze', *New Society* 21 August: 26.

Pollard, A. (1988) 'Controversial issues and reflective teaching', pp. 54–70 in B. Carrington and B. Troyna (eds) *Children and Controversial Issues: Strategies for the Early and Middle Years of Schooling*, Lewes: Falmer Press.

Randall, S. (1988) 'The New Right, racism and education in Thatcher's Britain', *Sage Race Relations Abstracts* 13 (3): 3–17.

Reeves, F. (1983) *British Racial Discourse*, Cambridge: Cambridge University Press.

Rex, J. and Tomlinson, S. (1979) *Colonial Immigrants in a British City: a Class Analysis*, London: Routledge & Kegan Paul.

Richardson, R. (1988) 'Opposition to reform and the need for transformation: some polemical notes', *Multicultural Teaching* 6 (2): 4–10.

Riley, K. (1982) 'Black girls speak for themselves', *Multiracial Education*, 10 (3): 3–12.

Rose, E.J.B. *et al.* (1969) *Colour and Citizenship: a Report on British Race Relations*, Oxford: Oxford University Press.

Royal Borough of Kensington and Chelsea (1989) *The Future of Education in the Royal Borough of Kensington and Chelsea*, London, February.

Scruton, R., Ellis-Jones, A. and O'Keefe, D. (1985) *Education and Indoctrination*, Harrow, Middlesex: Education Research Centre.

Select Committee on Race Relations and Immigration (1969) *The Problems of Coloured School Leavers*, London: HMSO.

Select Committee on Race Relations and Immigration (1977) *The West Indian Community*, Vol. 1, London: HMSO.

Sexton, S. (1988) 'Squeezing out choice at the grassroots', *Education* 9 September: 237.

Sharp, R. and Green, A. (1975) *Education and Social Control*, London: Routledge & Kegan Paul.

Shor, I. (1986) *Culture Wars*, London: Routledge & Kegan Paul.

Short, G. and Carrington, B. (1987) 'Towards an antiracist initiative in the all-white primary school' pp. 220–35 in A. Pollard (ed.) *Children and their Primary Schools: a New Perspective*, Lewes: Falmer Press.

Simon, B. (1984) 'Breaking school rules', *Marxism Today* September: 19–25.

Simon, B. (1988) *Bending the Rules*, London: Lawrence and Wishart.

Smith, D. (1977) *Racial Disadvantage in Britain*, Harmondsworth: Penguin.

Smith, D. and Tomlinson, S. (1989) *The School Effect: A Study of Multiracial Comprehensives*, London: Policy Studies Institute.

Solomos, J. (1988) *Black Youth, Racism and the State: the Politics of Ideology and Policy*, Cambridge: Cambridge University Press.

Street-Porter, R. (1978) *Race, Children and Cities* (Unit E361), Milton Keynes: Open University.

Taylor, B. (1986) 'Antiracist education in non-contact areas: the need for a gentle approach', *New Community* 13 (2): 177–84.

Thatcher, M. (1987) Speech to Annual Conservative Party

deficit" perspectives in contemporary educational research', *Comparative Education* 24 (3): 273-83.

Troyna, B. (1989) ' "A New Planet"? Tackling racial inequality in all-white schools and colleges', pp. 175 in G.K. Verma (ed.) *Education for All: A Landmark in Pluralism*, Lewes: Falmer Press.

Troyna, B. (1990) 'Reform or deform? The 1988 Education Reform Act and racial equality in Britain', *New Community* 16 (3).

Troyna, B. and Ball, W. (1985) *Views from the Chalk Face: School Responses to an LEA's Policy on Multicultural Education*, Policy Papers in Ethnic Relations No. 1, Coventry: University of Warwick, Centre for Research in Ethnic Relations. (Reprinted in 1987.)

Troyna, B. and Selman, L. (1989) 'Surviving in the "Survivalist Culture": anti-racist strategies and practice in the new ERA', *Journal of Further and Higher Education* 13 (2): 22-36.

Troyna, B. and Williams, J. (1986) *Racism, Education and the State: The Racialisation of Education Policy*, Beckenham: Croom Helm.

Tuck, D. (1988) 'Local financial management', *Educational Management and Administration* 16 (2): 140-8.

Verma, G.K. (ed.) (1989) *Education for All: A Landmark in Pluralism*, Lewes: Falmer Press.

Walker, S. and Barton, L. (eds) (1986) *Youth, Unemployment and Schooling*, Milton Keynes: Open University Press.

Wellman, D. (1977) *Portraits of White Racism*, Cambridge: Cambridge University Press.

Whitty, G. and Menter, I. (1989) 'Lessons of Thatcherism: education policy in England and Wales 1979-1988', *Journal of Law and Society* 16 (1): 42-64.

Widgery, D. (1986) *Beating Time*, London: Chatto & Windus.

Williams, J. (1986) 'Education and race: the racialisation of class inequalities?', *British Journal of Sociology of Education* 7 (2): 135-54.

Williams, J., Dunning, E. and Murphy, P. (1984) *Hooligans Abroad: The Behaviour and Control of English Fans in Continental Europe*, London: Routledge & Kegan Paul.

Williams, S. (1989) 'Foreward', pp. vii-ix in G.K. Verma (ed.)

kpool, 9 October.

Thatcher, [...] 8) Address to the General Assembly [...] land, Edinburgh, 21 May.

Church [...] 4) 'Principles of anti-racist education', *Cu[...]*

Thomas, B. [...] 2 (3): 20[...]hford, P., Burke, J., Farquhar, C. and Plewi[...]

Tizard, B., [...] *Children at School in the Inner City*, Ho[...] (1988) Y[...]baum Associates.

Lawrence [...] Tomlinson, S. (1981) *Educational Sub-normality*, London [...] Routle[...] & Kegan Paul.

Tomlinson, S. (1983) *Ethnic Minorities in British Schools*, London: Heinemann.

Tomlinson, S. (1987) 'Curriculum option choices in multi-ethnic schools', pp. 92–108 in B. Troyna (ed.) *Racial Inequality in Education*, London: Tavistock.

Tomlinson, S. (1989) 'Education and training', *New Community* 15 (3): 461–9.

Tracy, M. (1986) 'Initial teacher training and multicultural education', *Journal of Further and Higher Education* 10 (3): 67–75.

Troyna, B. (1979) 'Differential commitment to ethnic identity by black youths in Britain', *New Community* 7 (3): 406–14.

Troyna, B. (1982) 'The ideological and policy response to black pupils in British schools', pp. 127–43 in A. Hartnett (ed.) *The Social Sciences in Educational Studies*, London: Heinemann.

Troyna, B. (1984a) 'Fact or artefact: the "educational under-achievement" of black pupils', *British Journal of Sociology of Education* 5 (2): 153–66.

Troyna, B. (1984b) 'Multicultural education: emancipation or containment?', pp. 75–92 in L. Barton and S. Walker (eds) *Social Crisis and Educational Research*, Beckenham: Croom Helm.

Troyna, B. (1986) ' "Swann's Song": the origins, ideology and implications of *Education for All*', *Journal of Education Policy* 1 (2): 171–81. (Reprinted in T. Chivers [ed.] [1987].)

Troyna, B. (1987) 'Beyond multiculturalism: towards the enactment of anti-racist education in policy, provision and pedagogy', *Oxford Review of Education* 13 (3): 307–20.

Troyna, B. (1988) 'Paradigm regained: a critique of "cultural

Education for All: A Landmark in Pluralism, Lewes: Falmer Press.

Wright, C. (1987) 'Black students – white teachers', pp. 109–26 in B. Troyna (ed.) *Racial Inequality in Education*, London: Tavistock.

Yates, L. (1988) 'Does "all students" include girls? Some reflections on recent educational practice and theory', *Australian Educational Researcher* 15 (1): 41–57.

Yeomans, A. (1983) 'Collaborative group work in primary and secondary schools', *Durham and Newcastle Research Review* 10: 95–105.

Index